75-49556

Death in the Secular City

Death
in the
Secular City

LIFE AFTER DEATH
IN CONTEMPORARY
THEOLOGY
AND PHILOSOPHY

by RUSSELL ALDWINCKLE

WILLIAM B. EERDMANS PUBLISHING COMPANY
Grand Rapids, Michigan

© George Allen & Unwin Ltd. 1972
First published 1972. This American edition published
April 1974 by special arrangement with George Allen &
Unwin Ltd., London.

Printed in the United States of America

Library of Congress Cataloging in Publication Data

Aldwinckle, Russell Foster.
    Death in the secular city.

    Bibliography: p. 185
    1. Death.
    2. Future life.
    I. Title.
BT825.A36   1974   236'.2   74-757
ISBN 0-8028-1574-X

Acknowledgments

Grateful acknowledgment is made to the following publishers for their courtesy in permitting the quotation of brief extracts from copyright works: To Harper & Row, Publishers, Inc., New York, for permission to use quotations from *In the End, God,* by J. A. T. Robinson; to Charles Scribner's Sons, New York, for permission to use quotations from *Systematic Theology: A Historicist Perspective,* by Gordon Kaufman; to Crossroad Books, New York, for permission to use quotations from *Hope and History,* by Josef Pieper; and to the University of Chicago Press, Chicago, for permission to use quotations from *Systematic Theology,* by Paul Tillich.

Foreword

'It is appointed unto men once to die.' There are few statements in the Bible which will be as little disputed as this. There have from time to time been hysterical expectations of a second coming and a millennium on earth, and on occasion men have sought for some elixir of life which will remove the spectre of death from their path. Most of us consider these to be vain hopes. Modern biology does not take us, and is not likely to take us in a foreseeable future, beyond a very limited elongation of the natural span as men have found it down the ages. Three score years and ten is not too bad an expectation today as in the past. Sooner or later we all share the same fate. Life comes to its inevitable end.

Indeed, no one seriously doubts that in, let us say, twenty-five years a very large proportion of the people now living on this earth will be dead. This appears, in the main, to be a fact we are able to take with surprising equanimity. On the face of it, very few people seem to be seriously perturbed by having to live in this way under sentence of death. There are many reasons for this, and they can hardly be investigated closely in a short note like this one. But clearly one important factor is that, by some kindly gift of nature, though not all would so regard it, we are able to keep our awareness of the inevitability of death at the level of what Newman called 'notional' rather than 'real' belief. There is nothing we can do about it, beyond the little we may do to hold the Reaper at bay a while. So why bother? There is so much to do in the meantime, and the time is short. Moreover, though we know that the time is short, the uncertainty of the actual ending of one's life enables many, in their own case especially, to think of what is left as in fact very long and indefinite—we accord ourselves, as it were, a little private eternity, notwithstanding that, in another frame of mind, and as practical people, we make our wills— and put it all out of our minds as soon as we have done so. It is morbid to think too much about death, and most of us, I suspect, just forget it or think of it as so remote in our own case that we need not bother. There are, no doubt, deeper psychological levels at which this happy obliviousness may be more fully explained. But the fact remains that for many, in the absence of some untoward fate which is (so we think) less likely to happen to us than to others, life seems to stretch ahead without certain end. The months and the years pass very quickly, and in middle age the terms and the seasons 'fly' with relentless haste. No sooner is it summer than the leaves begin to turn for autumn. But not so life, it goes on—so we often think.

It would be wrong, however, to suppose that people take death with calmness just because they are able to put it out of their minds. It does strike, and we see friends and relatives go, sometimes grieving sorely as we miss them. Moreover, the imminence of a person's own death becomes inescapably clear in some cases, and there are many instances, some very notable ones, where the closeness of certain death seems to be taken with great serenity. At times this is due to religious faith. It is not thought that death is in fact 'the end'. For others this is combined, as in the famous case of Socrates, with stoical reasonableness. But there are others, and by no means always people whose lives have been dull or wretched, who are quite unperturbed by the thought that death is at the door. One of the most celebrated was David Hume. He was convinced, not only that it is unlikely that there will be anything after death, but that it is just not conceivable that we should exist in any way when the course of the present life is run. When his friend Boswell teased him somewhat gently about this on his death bed, he replied with very pleasant bantering in turn. Boswell's semi-serious pleasantries did not get him down. Nor is this happy acceptance confined to men of genius.

On the other hand, in a somewhat different vein, we are all apt to think of death as a great calamity. There are few fates 'worse than death'. The 'supreme penalty' is death, and one of the main reasons for the abolition of the death penalty is the extreme mental torment endured by those await it, some of them young and in the prime of life, as they see the days and the hours and the minutes slip by. When we read of an accident, or a flood or famine, we are much perturbed at the terrible 'toll of life' that has been taken. 'How terrible', we exclaim, 'what a waste'; and even though we have become almost fatalistically reconciled to war and rumours of war, we also think of it as one of the greatest of evils, not only because of the misery caused to the living and the evil passions engendered, but also because of the appalling loss of life. We likewise take a grave view of those who, by careless conduct, endanger the lives of others on the roads. Nor are there many crimes in history which distress us more than the slaughter of millions in recent times in concentration camps and gas-chambers, or the brutality of the killing of civilians as well as soldiers in Vietnam. Life is precious, death is the great enemy, the 'last enemy', cunningly and confidently lying in wait for us all.

Where, between these extremes and variations of mood, the ordinary citizen stands may not be very easy to determine. The day-to-day round of our lives may not give us the best clue. What we think 'at the top of our minds' may not be what we always feel 'at the bottom of our hearts'. In stressing this distinction, the late Professor John Baillie quoted as follows[1] from Thomas Hardy's diary: 'If all hearts were open and all desires known—as they would be if people showed their souls—how many gapings, sighings, clenched fists, knotted brows, broad grins, and red eyes would we see in the market-place.' Might we not find, 'if people showed their souls', that the thought of our ultimate dissolution affected us more deeply than is perhaps evident at first. Thomas Hobbes was a shrewd observer of human nature, and, atheist and severe critic of the Church that he was, he had no theological axe to grind. He held that deep in our motivations was the stark fear of death. His own temperament may have affected this judgment, and it is perhaps exaggerated as he understood it. But might we not find, 'if all hearts were open', that Hobbes was not as wide of the mark as all that? No particular piety or morbidity is needed to set us wondering whether death is in fact the end. If we think that it is, that need not mean that all is lost. Life still has its savour, there is much to accomplish in and for itself. The humanist does not give way to morose despair. All the same, it is very hard not to be troubled by the thought that, when our bodies are laid to rest (as we euphemistically put it), all that we attain, in skills, understanding, affection and virtue, is blotted out forever, except for its effects elsewhere. We cling also to the distinctiveness of our own being and that of others. Such indeed are the dominant themes of contemporary art and literature. The curious convolutions of character, failure of commitment alongside a passionate and humane sense of justice, privacy and the sense of 'inner emptiness', frustration and absurdity, the 'sombre solitude' of which Bertrand Russell, notwithstanding the liveliness and variety of his own contacts, complains—the variations on these and related themes, sometimes overtly and sometimes in more oblique and subtle ways, are suggestive of a need, indeed we might say a yearning, that may lie deep in the hearts of all for more than the passing scene, for some larger hope, a 'beyond'. 'Men at times are sober, and think by fits and starts.' When the sober fit is on, will not the thought of the transitoriness of our present achievements loom very large? Have we some reason to expect more?

It is with these questions that Professor Aldwinckle is concerned.

[1] *Our Knowledge of God*, p. 9.

The book is addressed to the layman as well as the scholar, and the author brings to it his own philosophical expertise as well as a deep and reflective Christian commitment. He knows how philosophy may help and what are its limits. He views his problems against the background of contemporary thought and the search for an adequate concept of persons; and the firmness with which he holds his own views is more impressive because of the patience and restraint with which he presents them. To have a clear, cultivated mind playing about these basic problems, as they present themselves to us today, is indeed a boon, and I hope therefore that this book will be widely read and pondered. It will be surprising if it is not.

H. D. LEWIS, B.LITT, M.A., D.D

Preface

The issue of personal immortality, interpreted as the survival of death, does not occupy a central or even near-central position in much contemporary Christian thinking. This book has been written in the conviction that the result has been to ignore one important dimension of the faith. We believe the time has come to swing back the pendulum and to remind even Christians that their hope is not confined to this world. Considerations of length have forced me at times to appear dogmatic on many issues which are still under vigorous debate. The point I wish to emphasize is that in spite of this, the present climate of thought, philosophical and theological, has changed so much as to make the discussion of the survival of death no longer the oddity it might have appeared only a few years ago.

Even a cursory reading will reveal the author's indebtedness to many, but I would like in particular to mention Professor H. D. Lewis of King's College, University of London, who read the whole manuscript and made valuable comments, and the Right Reverend Dr I. T. Ramsey, the present Bishop of Durham. Both have given generously of their time and interest over many years of valued friendship. While they cannot be held responsible for the views expressed, it is clear that their written work and personal conversation have deeply influenced me in the way I have tried to tackle this difficult theme. Finally a tribute of admiration and gratitude to two other men who shaped my thinking on this and other topics in the days of my youth when I first started upon serious theological study. They are the late Dr H. Wheeler Robinson, then Principal of Regent's Park College, just moved to Oxford, and Professor Oscar Cullmann of the Protestant Faculty of the University of Strasbourg, who was my teacher and friend in that historic and beautiful city.

I would like also to thank the Board of Trustees of McMaster Divinity College for making possible a half-year sabbatical in Oxford where most of the research was done, and the Principal and tutors of Regent's Park College for giving me the privileges of the Senior Common-room and a quiet place in which to think and write. It would also be ungracious not to mention the stimulus of generations of students at McMaster who, by their ruthless questioning, have compelled me, for good or ill, to try and clarify my own convictions.

My son David has engaged me in vigorous discussion from time to time on this theme and given me whatever understanding I may have of what is going on in the minds of the younger generation. One never writes even a small book in splendid isolation. My wife has had to live with the manuscript too, and to her I express my thanks, which go far beyond the limits of the academic.

RUSSELL ALDWINCKLE
The Divinity School
McMaster University
Hamilton, Ontario, 1971

Contents

Chapter One

Last Things First

Some years ago Dr Gordon Rupp wrote a little book which bore the title which I have stolen for the heading of this chapter.[1] Perhaps he will excuse this plagiarism as a tribute to friendship started many years ago in Strasbourg and as an expression of appreciation of the contents of that book. After his insistence that eschatology should not be treated as the Cinderella of Christian doctrine, the following sentence occurs in his book: 'To speak of an immortality of the race, of something which persists though the individual perishes, is in the end a bitter sentimentalism.'[2] The reader of this present work is asked to keep this firmly in mind in what follows. It may serve as a kind of text to remind us continually of what the real issues are. Without in any way suggesting that Dr Rupp would agree with everything in the present work, my intention is at least to justify and give fresh emphasis to the point of view he has so well expressed.

It seems to be the fate of Christian theology to swing from one position to another without achieving for very long a stable and balanced equilibrium. The thinkers of the Church have tried again and again to reach such a balanced synthesis of elements, only to find the 'system' broken up again by new forces and pressures. Some will contend that this only proves that because man is essentially a historical being, the dynamic factors involved in the process of becoming must always overcome the static. All progress, theological or otherwise, depends upon this constant disintegration of former patterns of thought which have become too rigid and which no longer speak relevantly to a world in which new forces are at work. In a sense this may be true, and we have to live with it. However, it only emphasizes the necessity from time to time to swing back the pendulum to restore the balance and to preserve truths which are in grave danger of being forgotten.

I believe that we live in such a period and that the Christian Church

[1] E. G. Rupp, *Last Things First*.
[2] ibid., p. 57.

needs to consider again with great urgency the question of the fate and destiny of the individual beyond this world of time and space. It is well known that at the last meeting of the World Council of Churches at Uppsala in Sweden in 1968, there was considerable tension below the surface, sometimes erupting into open expression, between the radical 'activists' and those who liked to think of themselves as standing for the full gospel once delivered to the saints and handed on to us through the worship, creeds and traditions of some branch of institutional Christianity. As usual, the alternatives offered to us by the extremists do not constitute a simple 'either-or'. The activists did sometimes give the impression that their interest was concentrated exclusively on peace, justice, poverty, race and other problems. It was not always clear whether they believed that the Christian gospel had any other dimension than this or whether it was indeed important at all. For some, it did not seem to matter whether anything was affirmed about the ultimate destiny and salvation of the individual provided the Church acted in relation to Vietnam, Biafra, race and other issues which tormented the world and Christian opinion at the time when the World Council met. We can agree that this concern with social issues was not entirely new. Indeed, it is one of the myths held by the present generation of social reformers that they have discovered this aspect of the Christian gospel for the first time. Any acquaintance with the nineteenth century and the present century before the World Council came into being in 1947 would give the lie to this assumption. Of course, it has always been true that many Christians, not to mention the masses of people in general, have been relatively indifferent to some or all of these issues. This is equally true of the present generation.

The time does seem to have come, however, to take stock and have a good hard look at this emphasis upon the social dimension of the Christian faith. We agree that there can be no love of God which does not involve love of neighbour. There can be no question of the Church turning its back upon its responsibilities in this world. The fact remains none the less that this is not the whole gospel. There is another side of Christian truth which has a word to speak about the ultimate destiny of the individual. Indeed, it could well be argued that the decay of strong convictions on this latter point is also undermining the stamina and patience of Christians and others in the fulfilling of their social obligations here and now. Despite the oft-repeated gibe about 'pie in the sky', it is not in fact true that the hope of heaven has always inhibited the dynamic energy for social change in the present. In the long history of the Christian Church, some forms of radical other-worldliness may justly be charged with this neglect of mundane affairs. On the other hand, numerous exceptions must also be taken into account, ranging through the centuries up to the pioneers of the anti-slavery movements of modern times and to the social gospel of men like William Temple and Walter Rauschenbusch, to name only two.

We shall be concerned in this work almost exclusively with questions concerning the destiny of the individual beyond death. Let it be repeated again that this is not a dismissal of the Christian's responsibilities in this world. Our concentration upon it springs from the conviction that the neglect of this question concerning the future of the individual is a profound weakness of much contemporary Christian life, particularly in the West. Its repercussions are deep and far-reaching and may have much to do with a certain spiritual lassitude which seems to afflict even the most well-intentioned Christians of today, not to mention secular man himself. It is not suggested that belief in the personal survival of death has completely disappeared from the contemporary Christian consciousness. If the ordinary grass-roots church member were asked whether this was an essential article of the Christian faith, he would no doubt say yes. He would be hard put to it to say exactly how he understood it or whether he was in favour of resurrection or immortality. Nevertheless, in a vague and general sense he would probably want to affirm it. It is also true that many Christians today, while not denying an after-life, would tend to play down its importance. They would not feel that it played any decisive role in their behaviour as Christians here and now. If it is true, so much the better, but the important thing is to act now in the spirit of Christ and leave the future in the hands of God where it properly belongs. At first sight, this seems very proper and even very pious. Yet on closer examination, we may well wonder whether this comparative indifference to personal survival is not bound up with deep and gnawing doubts about God and His purpose for men's future.

The contemporary situation, however, is characterized by another factor which is comparatively new. From the eighteenth century onwards, we have become accustomed to the outright denial of personal survival of death by sceptical philosophers, materialistic scientists, positivists, some philosophical analysts, humanists, naturalists, and Marxists. This is not surprising, given their general view of the world and the nature of man. What is striking at the present time is the degree to which thinkers who claim to be Christian have capitulated to this modern mood and seek to interpret the gospel in purely this-worldly terms. The purpose of this rather extended essay is to examine again the basic issues concerning the destiny of the individual and to give a careful scrutiny to certain important theological expressions of the gospel for this world only.

It also seems to be the fate of Christian thought in our age to live by slogans and labels. No doubt the rapid dissemination of ideas via the paperback and the electronic media is in part responsible for this. We had neo-orthodoxy after 1918, various forms of existentialism, demythologizing, the 'God is dead' slogan, the new hermeneutics and now the theology of hope. It is the fundamental contention of this book that there is no real theology of hope if the individual's final end is to be extinction. Unless modern Christianity can recover a faith in the kind of God who is both able and willing to rescue His children from the last enemy, death, any other hope promised must be precarious, short-lived and doomed to increasing impairment under the pressures of human life and history as we experience them here and now. To most Christians of previous ages, this would have seemed a self-evident implication of the Christian faith, hardly deserving special emphasis unless they were engaged in debate with unbelievers. This, however, is emphatically not the case today. What distinguishes the present period is not the denial of survival by unbelievers. There is nothing new about that. It is the changed attitude of Christians themselves to this question, and it is this which we propose to examine.

It is not suggested that all those associated with the 'theology of hope' are concerned only with human life in this world. As usual, any imposition of a label in an undiscriminating way must be both prejudiced and unfair in regard to particular thinkers. The fact remains, however, that much contemporary discussion of Christian hope is directed almost exclusively to considerations relevant to mankind's future on this planet or perhaps in the distant galaxies. We say 'mankind's future' because it is obvious when one stops to think about it that millions of individuals now living and countless generations who have gone before us will have no conscious participation in these long-term hopes, if indeed they are ever realized in this world.

It would not, of course, be correct to say that there is no concern with death in the Western world. We are so hypnotized by such phrases as 'man come of age' and 'the secular city' that we are all too apt to assume that the majority of people today live in a highly sophisticated intellectual atmosphere. For good or ill, this is just not so. In fact, our Western culture is a curious mixture of sophistication, sentimentality and sheer superstition. In many ways, it begins to take on a peculiar resemblance to the Graeco-Roman world in which the Christian faith had to win its way in the early centuries of our era. The continuing popularity of certain religious sects with their emphasis on the near end of the world proves that there are millions who do not accept the 'secular' label. Modern enlightenment does not prevent the growth of animal cemeteries and the quasi-religious sentimentality which attaches to them. Spiritualism still has a larger following than most of us want to acknowledge. The widespread interest in astrology and horoscopes, even when only half-believed, shows that not all have 'come of age'. It may, of course, be the lack of any positive note struck by Christians in regard to personal survival which accounts for these attempts to fill the void.

When we pass from what sociologists sometimes call rather disparagingly 'sub-cultures' to those who regard themselves as the intellectual elite of our time, we find much concern with death. After all, was it not Heidegger who accustomed us to think of man as a being-toward-death (*Sein zum Tode*) and to define authentic existence as the honest and courageous living of our lives in the frank recognition of this fact? To see my life from the standpoint of my ultimate death and ceasing to be is the foundation of all courage and clear vision of life's possibilities.[1] For Sartre, human freedom must be exercised in a world where God is dead and death for man is the final end. This is the true absurdity. We may, however, be grateful to the continental existentialists for compelling us to face the reality of personal death without glossing it over with vague and utopian social ideals cast into an indefinite future. Dr Milton Gatch has recently given us an illuminating study of the role of death in such novelists as Thomas Mann, Tolstoy and Albert Camus.[2] Another treatment of death in twentieth-century fiction by Eric Rhode is to be found in a recent volume edited by Arnold Toynbee.[3] A few years ago Jacques Choron wrote on death and Western thought.[4] We are all familiar with recent discussions by medical men concerning the exact medical definition of death, a subject that has now become of more than academic interest in the light of heart transplant surgery.

[1] M. Heidegger, *Being and Time*; J. Wild, *The Challenge of Existentialism*, pp. 118–19.
[2] M. McC. Gatch, *Death-Meaning and Mortality in Christian Thought and Contemporary Culture*.
[3] Arnold Toynbee and Others, *Man's Concern with Death*.
[4] J. Choron, *Death and Western Thought*.

What is striking is that in the midst of so much concern about death both in contemporary literature and modern medicine, the Christian voice has been strangely muted. Not often do we hear from the Christian Church today the triumphant challenge of the apostle: 'O death, where is thy sting? O grave, where is thy victory?' The modern Christian often seems strangely silent and even indifferent, at least on the surface. One can never be absolutely sure as to what goes on in the deep recesses of a man's soul. Perhaps it is true, as has often been said in recent years, that the most significant modern repression is not sex, as with the Victorians, but death. David Edwards reminds us that Freud confessed that he thought about death every day of his life.[1] At the present moment, if we wish to find significant reflections upon death, we must, at least in America or Britain, either go to the 'God is dead' group or to the philosophers of religion. The former can hardly be expected to speak very positively of life after death in view of their attitude to the question concerning God's reality. In philosophy, in the Anglo-Saxon world, the position is somewhat different. Despite the prevalent misconception that modern philosophy in Britain and the United States is synonymous with certain schools of empiricism and philosophical analysis, this is by no means the case. There is already impressive evidence that a 'new revolution' in philosophy has begun in quite a different sense from that associated with Gilbert Ryle. The publication of H. D. Lewis's *The Elusive Mind*, with its powerful defence of the irreducible distinction between physical and mental reality, is indeed a landmark.[2] His vigorous attack upon the prevailing fashions of thought and his defence of a spiritual 'self' and even the possibility of a genuine personal immortality show that philosophers may once more be starting to discuss those fundamental questions of human destiny which have always concerned the ordinary man and woman.

As far as the Western theological tradition is concerned, there was until recently much concern with this question of death and man's possible victory over it. It is clearly seen in such liberal theologians as Harnack and Canon Streeter. The Reformed tradition, when faithful to Luther and Calvin, certainly had much to say. Barth and Brunner, between the two world wars and for some years afterwards, continued to speak about resurrection and man's eternal destiny after death. European continental theology has never lost this emphasis and is powerfully represented by younger theologians such as Pannenberg

[1] D. L. Edwards, *The Last Things Now*, p. 12.
[2] H. D. Lewis, *The Elusive Mind*.

and Moltmann. Roman Catholic theology has always had much to say about life after death and still does so when it is loyal to its ancient symbols of faith and its theological tradition. The last decade, however, has seen a marked change of emphasis among some of the younger thinkers in both Catholicism and Protestantism. It may be said that these are still only a minority and do not speak for the *consensus fidelium* of the churches to which they belong. This may be true, but their influence may grow, and in so far as they confirm many hesitant believers in their already strongly this-worldly orientation, they may well be the voice of the future. On the other hand, they may be leading modern Christianity to a dead end in more senses than one, where a true word of hope can no longer be spoken to man when he faces the reality of his own death.

It is with these tendencies that we shall be primarily concerned. There are, of course, many Christian thinkers still who affirm as strongly as ever personal survival of death. It is the others, however, who often have the ear of the young and who often appear to evoke the most enthusiastic assent. It is because the young are certain to be sadly disillusioned sooner or later with an exclusively this-worldly version of the Christian faith that it is imperative to speak now, however feebly, in the attempt to redress the balance. It may seem hopelessly quixotic and indeed obscurantist to try and interest the young in life after death when so many pressing problems need to be dealt with now. Yet human aspirations and yearnings can never be satisfied for ever with crusades against pollution and social injustice, necessary as these are and in their true perspective, the proper objects of Christian sacrificial concern here and now. It is part of our contention that a superficial 'either-or' is not the only option of the Christian for the future. It does not follow that the hope of heaven necessarily means that one is against earth, however one-sided some Christians have been in the past. In a truly Christian and not a cynical sense, the case can be made that one of the glories of the Christian faith is that a man can have the best of both worlds. The present world, with all its possibilities, is after all God's world. What comes after death is also in His hands. The Christian hope spans both time and eternity and we should not opt for less.

There is another aspect to this question which has been well expressed by Bonhoeffer, and that is the psychological effect upon men of the conviction that death is really the end. It is often considered to be a libel to assert that if men do not believe in a life after death, they will eat, drink and be merry, for tomorrow they die. The fact remains, however, that the finality of death can also evoke a frantic attempt to squeeze as much out of this life as possible in the shortest period of time, since no man knows when the bell will toll for him. This has been powerfully stated by Bonhoeffer in his *Ethics* in a passage which I take leave to quote in full:

The miracle of Christ's resurrection makes nonsense of that idolization of death which is prevalent among us today. Where death is the last thing, fear of death is combined with defiance. Where death is the last thing, earthly life is all or nothing. Boastful reliance on earthy eternities goes side by side with a frivolous playing with life. A convulsive acceptance and seizing hold of life stands cheek by jowl with indifference and contempt for life.[1]

It is not enough to dismiss this with contempt as a Christian distortion or to say that men ought to accept death as perfectly natural and die with quiet and serene acquiescence. Bonhoeffer has put his finger on a sensitive spot which contemporary man may consciously refuse to face. There is much, however, in the feverish modern search for intense experiences in this present life which gives impressive support to his analysis of our situation.

No man has written more movingly about death as the final end of man than the late Bertrand Russell. His long and remarkable career has deeply impressed more than one generation. More than any other single man, particularly in the English-speaking countries, he has been responsible for the modern distrust of human desires. His influence and Freud's have helped to implant in countless modern men and women the almost morbid and pathological fear of being victims of wishful thinking. For many, Christian hopes have become just too good to be true. We feel more honest with sober and chastened hopes. No doubt contemporary history, with its war, violence and strife, has been a large factor too in depressing human hope, as far as the after-life is concerned. So many this-worldly hopes have had to be deferred to an indefinite future that it seems absurd to throw them into an existence after death. This seems to be true despite the influence of spiritualism after each of the world wars and its continuing appeal to relatively small groups of people, including such notable people as Sir Oliver Lodge in England after the First World War and Bishop Pike in the USA in more recent years.

Another facet of the same question has been emphasized by Teilhard

[1] D. Bonhoeffer, *Ethics* (ed. E. Bethge), p. 16.

de Chardin when he says that 'the great enemy of the modern world, "Public Enemy No. 1" is boredom.'[1] He rightly points out that as long as men are preoccupied with securing the basic material necessities of life, this is not a major problem. This is still the case with millions in the non-Western world and probably with considerable sections in our so-called affluent society. Nevertheless, where modern technology has successfully freed men from the immediate fear of starvation and disease and given them increased leisure, there are already signs that they are beginning to experience the 'first pangs of taedium vitae'. 'Despite all appearances, Mankind is bored. Perhaps this is the underlying cause of all our troubles . . . We no longer know what to do with ourselves.'[2] The more leisure men have to reflect upon the meaning of life, the more important is the threat of death likely to become. We are no longer too busy to think about it. There is every reason to think that this issue will become more pressing rather than less. In any case, it is imperative for Christians to ask again what, if anything, the Christian faith has to say about this problem. We agree with Carl Braaten:

If man is to hope for individual, personal fulfilment, in some sense he must hope for life after death, for he knows that such fulfilment cannot occur within the limits of this earthly existence. The question whether hope can survive cannot ultimately disregard whether there is something to hope for that transcends death, the last hindrance to life.[3]

[1] T. De Chardin, *The Future of Man*, p. 145.
[2] ibid., p. 146.
[3] M. E. Marty, and D. G. Peerman, *New Theology no. 5*, p. 103.

Chapter Two

Science and Man's Future

It is a curious feature about much theological writing about the Christian hope and man's future, whether in this world or beyond, that it ignores the pressing questions which arise from our scientific understanding of the world. Much stress is put upon man's increasing control over the forces of nature as the result of scientific progress and its technological application. More and more man seems to be gaining effective control over himself and his environment. By 'over himself', I do not mean that man shows more capacity to bring his unruly desires and appetites under moral and spiritual discipline. It would be very difficult to make out a convincing case for that. Rather am I thinking of the power to manipulate his body and his psychological reactions. Such control ranges all the way from the shaping of his genetic development to the conditioning of his behaviour and attitudes by physiological and psychological changes brought about by the human will. To this must be added the social conditioning of human beings by the exploitation of psychological methods such as the conditioned reflex and the power of suggestion. Also, no doubt, the use of drugs should be included. It is curious that at a time when many assume that science has rendered impossible the very idea of the survival of death by individual persons, it is believed by many that science has given the human race an unlimited lease of life in this present space-time existence. It is highly doubtful, however, whether science can be successfully invoked in defence of this latter point.

This power, which man has acquired, only renders more pressing the importance of human decisions and even more the scale of moral and spiritual values which will influence him as he seeks to mould the man of the future. In their sharp reaction against an other-world-liness which despises this world as a vale of tears and which serves only as a prelude to the eternal realm, the modern 'theologians of hope' often speak as if man has unlimited time ahead of him in which to solve the tension between the possession of enormous power and its proper use. It is assumed, if accidents are avoided and the nuclear holocaust does not occur, that the cosmic process will continue indefinitely and that there are no limits to what man may achieve within the present spatial and temporal order of which he is a part. There is, however, a curious contradiction here between this optimistic account of man's future possibilities and the cautious forecasts of the scientists themselves. It is important to distinguish between the psychological and the theological and philosophical issues. Obviously, from the perspective of the individual life of three score years and ten, even a thousand years from now seems a long way off. If the disappearance of life from this part of the cosmos were to take place in many billions of years from now, this would leave most men unaffected. We would go about our business instead of brooding about our distant fate. This is in fact what most people do, and no doubt they are wise in their own way so to act. However, as Teilhard de Chardin has reminded us, the more intelligent and reflective men become under the pressure of scientific progress and the more they are influenced by the scientific picture of man's place in nature, the more difficult they will find it to evade this question of man's long-term future in space and time. When Christians join hands with Marxists in speaking in glowing terms about our future in this world, they too can hardly avoid this question.

It is one of the frequent criticisms of nineteenth-century liberal theology that it was infected wtih a naive and ill-founded optimism which is supposed to have characterized that period. Whether the Victorian era as a whole was as confident about the future as is often supposed, it is certainly possible to select some utterances from the writers and thinkers of that era which express their hopes in the most extravagant manner.[1] It is equally certain that after 1918 there was a powerful reaction in Western society against such theories of inevitable progress. While it is true that American society probably felt the impact of this reversal of attitude somewhat later than Europe, the course of world history since 1918 has only confirmed many thoughtful Americans in their distrust of such optimism. The implications of this for Christian theology have also been far-reaching. In England between 1918 and 1939, Dean Inge gained considerable notoriety for his unrelenting attack upon the dogma of inevitable progress. In a famous essay entitled 'The Idea of Progress', the Dean of St Paul's employed his not inconsiderable wit to lambast the popular error. 'The Greeks prided themselves on being the degenerate descendants

[1] W. E. Houghton, *The Victorian Frame of Mind, 1830–1870.*

27

of gods, we on being the very creditable descendants of monkeys.'[1] While he did not dispute the advance in 'accumulating knowledge and experience and the instruments of living', he went on record as convinced that these things did not constitute 'real progress in human nature itself'.[2] In the absence of such 'real' progress, the other gains remain external and precarious. It is only fair to the 'gloomy Dean' to add that he held that the path of progress, that is of true intellectual, moral and spiritual development of the individual, was always open. It is clear, however, that he was decidedly cautious about predicting any widespread and universal 'progress' of this kind for the whole human race in the near future.

From a very different theological perspective than that of Inge's Christian Platonism, Reinhold Niebuhr, in the period between the two world wars and after, was attacking American optimism in the name of original sin and guilt. He was not advocating a return to a literal interpretation of the Genesis narratives or an acceptance of Augustinian theology as a whole. However, for Niebuhr, the 'myths' of the fall and of original sin contained true and permanently valid insights into the nature of human existence. The practical implications of this for the Christian understanding of history were important. While the Christian must work for a society in which more and more approximation will be made to social justice and the creation of conditions in which the Christian valuation of the person can flourish, it must never be forgotten that all advances in culture and civilization only reveal the essential ambiguities of power, as exercised in actual historical societies known to us. We must resolutely refuse to be hypnotized by the appeal of earthly utopias falsely identified with the kingdom of God upon earth. This in turn demands a crucial re-examination of the American dream of a new society no longer afflicted by the corruption of power and the injustice which marked the old Europe. Niebuhr's own hope for the future was a chastened one. He quotes with approval a remark of that notable Roman Catholic layman, Baron von Hügel, that ideally the Christian faith strives for a balance of 'sufficient otherworldliness without fanaticism and a sufficient thisworldliness without Philistinism'.[3] After admitting that much can be done to soften the incongruities and injustices of life on earth by a wise use of scientific power, he is driven to conclude: 'But all such strategies cannot finally overcome the fragmentary character

[1] W. R. Inge, *Outspoken Essays* (Second Series), p. 158 f.
[2] ibid., p. 175.
[3] R. Niebuhr, *The Irony of American History*, p. 44.

of human existence. The final wisdom of life requires, not the annulment of incongruity but the achievement of serenity within and above it.'[1] The more recent thinkers, whom we have mentioned in the last chapter, would no doubt be tempted to dismiss Niebuhr as representing a kind of tired cynicism from which they are only too anxious to escape. Jewish atheists such as Steve Weissman even suggest that, whether with deliberate intent or not, the 'Niebuhrian pessimism served the wielders of power during the Eisenhower years.'[2] Without committing ourselves to the total acceptance of the Niebuhr attitude, it may very well turn out to be the case that he did in fact recover a genuine insight about the nature of human existence in this world with which the more recent 'theologies of hope' will have to come to terms if their perspective is not to be unbelievably shallow and superficial.

For the present, however, it seems to be the case that many are in open revolt against the so-called pessimism of an Inge or a Niebuhr. There seems to be a desperate striving to recover an optimistic hope about man's future in this world. William Hamilton has told us that 'one of the motifs of the radical theology is its interest in the move from pessimism to optimism in American culture today'.[3]

Bertrand Russell, some years ago now, expressed eloquently in *A Free Man's Worship* his conviction that we must honestly face the ultimate and total extinction of the human race and yet continue to live our lives on the basis of unyielding despair. We must defy the cosmic forces which will eventually destroy us in the name of our highest values of justice and compassion, even though we know that such values can only have a temporary and fleeting embodiment until the final darkness descends. One can only respect the honesty and frankness of this position, however inadequate we may feel it to be. The Marxist may claim to be as realistic as this in his exclusive concentration upon this world, though there is little evidence that the Marxist elite have acquainted the toiling masses with their ultimate fate with the brutal frankness of a Russell. One might wonder how far the Marxist faith would survive among the proletariat if and when such an intellectual awakening takes place among them.

However, the question must be faced—have we any reason to believe that this present cosmos is eternal and that, although all individuals must face the annihilation of death, life itself will continue

[1] R. Niebuhr, *The Irony of American History*, p. 63.
[2] M. E. Marty and D. G. Peerman, *New Theology*, no. 5, p. 24.
[3] T. J. J. Altizer and W. Hamilton, *Radical Theology and the Death of God*, p. 156; cf. also p. 169.

to triumph and progress through the vast stretches of stellar space? Now that we have landed a man on the moon and may go even further afield, may we not look forward to an infinite living-space or *Lebensraum* in a universe without limit? Bernard Shaw once expressed this hope with poetic eloquence in his play *Back to Methuselah*:

Of Life only is there no end; and though of its million starry mansions many are empty and many still unbuilt and though its vast domain is as yet unbearably desert, my seed shall one day fill it and master its matter to its uttermost confines. And for what may be beyond, the eyesight of Lilith is too short. It is enough that there is a beyond.[1]

At the end of the nineteenth and in the early part of this century, there was a good deal of discussion about the implications of the law of entropy or the second law of thermodynamics. It seemed to some that if the physicists were right in believing that once energy has been expended, there cannot be a return to the initial state of affairs, then the universe is running down to a dead level of uniform heat. When this stage is reached, there will be no movement or activity and biological life will cease. Since the physicist can give no reason why energy was distributed in the first place in such a way as to make possible the cosmic process and movement in which we live, he can offer no further reason why the process could be reversed once the running-down of the universe has taken place. When this problem of entropy first dawned upon reflective minds, it produced in some, apocalyptic visions of the heat-death of the universe. Literary men such as Henry Adams wrote to William James that 'the universe has been terribly narrowed by thermodynamics'.[2] Others spoke of history and sociology as 'gasping for breath'.

We today pride ourselves on being much more cautious than the liberal theologians of the earlier period in trying to fit the Christian faith into a scientific cosmology which might at any moment be superseded by another. Scientists have warned us against making premature deductions from scientific theories. They themselves have suggested that the law of entropy only has precise meaning in relation to closed physical systems and that, therefore, we are in no position to extrapolate the principle and apply it to the universe as a whole. Oliver Lodge, as far back as 1931, declared to the British Association that the heat-death of the universe was a 'bugbear, an idol, to which philosophers need not bend the knee'. Professor Millikan referred to

---

[1] B. Shaw, *Back to Methuselah*, pp. 314–15.
[2] E. Meyerson, *De L'Explication dans des Sciences*, pp. 203 ff.

it as a dogma.[1] Recently Stephen Toulmin has given his view that to apply the law of thermodynamics in support of eschatological or philosophical doctrines is to misapply it. Since the law can only be stated in terms of 'thermally isolated systems' and since we cannot know whether the universe as a whole is such a system, we cannot be satisfied that there is any warrant in physics for the idea of the whole universe coming to a stop.[2] Astronomers have come up with new theories about a 'steady state' universe which involves neither a beginning in time nor a heat-death at the end.[3] Fred Hoyle has suggested the continuous creation of matter without attempting to clarify what creation here implies. He seems prepared to accept it with what Wordsworth called 'natural piety'. He admits, however, that without it 'the universe must evolve towards a dead state in which all the matter is condensed into a vast number of dead stars.'[4] Ian Barbour has commented: 'Both theories push explanation back to an unexplained situation which is treated as a "given": the primeval nucleus in Gamow's case, the "continual creation" of matter in Hoyle's. The question of the creation of time (finite or infinite) is not raised by either theory.'[5]

There were, of course, Christians like Dean Inge who argued that if the universe was running down, then it must have been wound up in the first place. He offered theism as the most 'rational' account of the facts uncovered by scientific investigation. Theologians such as Karl Barth, from a very different theological perspective, have emphasized the disastrous results in the past when faith has been tied up with passing metaphysical or scientific world-views. Even so, it is difficult to imagine any man reflecting upon the future of the human race and ignoring what the scientist has to say. But what has all this to do with hope, Christian or otherwise? For Christians who were able to affirm an eternal and transcendent God, it was not as shattering as might be expected. Nurtured on the Bible, they were not surprised to hear that man 'is as the grass of the field'. They could say with Emily Brontë:

Though earth and man were gone,
And suns and universes cease to be,
And Thou wert left alone,
Every existence would exist in Thee.

[1] E. A. Milne, *Modern Cosmology and the Christian Idea of God.*
[2] A. Macintyre (ed.), *Metaphysical Beliefs*, p. 25.
[3] E. L. Mascall, *Christian Theology and Natural Science*, p. 142.
[4] F. Hoyle, *The Nature of the Universe*, p. 110.
[5] I. G. Barbour, *Issues in Science and Religion*, p. 367.

This solution is not open to the more radical 'God is dead' theologian, particularly if the slogan is interpreted to signify not a contemporary psychological mood but a metaphysical and theological denial of the reality of the transcendent God.

But what of the continuing existence of this present world? Even if it is agreed that entropy has not spoken the last word about the universe, and that for all practical purposes the future of man seems to be spread out endlessly before him, can we really build an enduring hope on the assumption of the everlastingness of the present cosmos. It is well known that Aquinas was willing to concede the point that from a strictly philosophical point of view, the world might be eternal. He would also have maintained that even if this were the case, it would still have required a transcendent God to originate it and sustain it in being. The idea of a beginning and end to the world was a deduction from Scripture, not a philosophical or scientific necessity of thought. Whatever view we take on this particular issue, problems arise which can hardly be avoided when the future and man's hope for his own future is under consideration. Even if we try to combine theism and some doctrine of the eternity of the world, the fate of the individual person still remains an issue. Unless we have a doctrine of resurrection to a new life under conditions of space and time as we know them, then we have to face the fact that millions of human beings, past, present and future, are not going to share directly in the goal to which the whole creation moves—unless, of course, the individual's future is guaranteed in a realm not subject to death, and therefore beyond space and time. It is, however, this recourse to an eternal realm which is so distasteful to many contemporary writers about hope, even some Christian ones.

It is not quite clear where Whitehead and his philosophical and theological followers stand on this issue. Presumably the process does go on for ever. We shall have occasion later in our discussion of time to insist that it is quite legitimate to speak of God's continuous creativity, even after the end of the world as this is conceived in the New Testament eschatology. Since it is in doubt, however, whether God for Whitehead is personal, and certain that he did not advocate a form of personal immortality involving the existence of real persons after death, the basic problem remains. What of the ultimate destiny of the millions of people who are 'occasions' in this never-ending process of creative becoming but who will never live to experience a maturing of their moral and spiritual personalities? Surviving only in God's memory, whatever that may mean, still leaves the fundamental issues unresolved.[1] In any case, in the absence of any real personal existence after death, most of us must find our satisfaction in working for a goal we shall never live to see and our hope will be, not for ourselves, but for our very distant grandchildren. It might be argued that this is nobler than being inspired by convictions about one's future personal destiny. Be this as it may, the facts would have to be faced if these were really the facts. One would certainly like to know exactly where present writers on 'hope' stand on such issues as these.

It is curious that in view of the present emphasis upon the human future in this world, the ancient Christian doctrine of the millennium should receive such scant interest and respect from contemporary Christian thinkers. Whatever reservations we may have about its biblical exegesis or the way in which it interprets the eschatological symbols, or its frequent mistaken attempts to predict the end of the world, the millennial hope was certainly for a rule of God on this earth. This should appeal to many of our contemporaries. It could also be argued that the millennialists were more realistic than the moderns since, although they hoped for an earthly kingdom, they did not envisage it as eternal. It would eventually be taken up into the transcendent realm beyond space and time. This seems to be in substance the position of Teilhard de Chardin. Though he does not cast his future hopes into a millennial form, he does seem to envisage the perfect society, which is the goal of evolution, as being translated at the omega point to an eternal realm. When he moves beyond a scientific account of the omega, he tells us that 'if by its very nature [i.e. the omega], it did not escape from the time and space which it gathers together, it would not be the omega.'[2] These views certainly do not involve putting all our eggs into the earthly basket.

It is also worth pointing out that language about a 'new heaven and a new earth' does not invalidate the point. If the word 'new' in this kind of imagery is taken with real seriousness and if, in the renewed world, death, as we know it, has disappeared, then for all practical purposes we would be in a world so radically different from the one we know that we might just as well speak of a transcendent or eternal realm, that is a realm beyond the present order of the world as we now experience it. It seems to me, therefore, that we cannot avoid the basic question of the ultimate fate of the individual. This is not a matter of refined selfishness. If my existence is not worth preserving, even when

---

[1] As an interesting attempt to combine Christian and Whiteheadian ideas, cf. J. B. Cobb (Jr), *A Christian Natural Theology*.

[2] T. De Chardin, *The Phenomenon of Man*, p. 270.

God's grace has renewed and transformed it, then all other selves are in the same boat. It is cold comfort to insist that the Christian hope is for salvation of life in community informed by agape-love if multitudes of men and women are going to be excluded from such a love-feast! A 'theology of hope' must speak to these facts if it is to make sense even to secular and 'come of age' moderns. The only logical alternative would seem to be the realism of a Bertrand Russell.

The same comments are pertinent to the Marxist this-worldly eschatology. Again, it is well known that Marx spoke in almost lyrical terms of the classless society when the state and its corruptions of power would wither away. Few of us really believe that this happy state of affairs is going to happen in our lifetime. Even the student activists of this generation will have to face this unpleasant fact sooner or later. It could, of course, be argued that this is irrelevant. Since there is no God, there is no other option. Either we relapse into hopeless and passive resignation or we continue to work toward a better earthly goal, even if we never live to see its full implementation, and even if it is never realised at all. So be it. This again is the courage of ultimate despair. Nor can Christians refute its logic if the holders of this view cannot be enabled to see what the Christian believes can be seen of the workings of the transcendent God in the realm of human history. The Christian is often criticized for his 'pie in the sky'. At least let not the Marxist or even the humanist pretend about the future. Let him at least work for the future with his eyes fully open. Let him not delude the faithful with promises which will never be fulfilled on this earth, or even on some distant planet colonised by a new race of space-men. Dean Inge once had some caustic remarks about turning the lovely countryside of England's Essex into East and West Ham. It is difficult to get excited about the proliferation of four lane highways, hot-dog stands, films of violence and sex on Jupiter and Mars or some other globe in our galactic region. Some will no doubt angrily reply that this is ridiculous abuse and no serious argument. Not so! It puts, crudely perhaps, the gnawing doubt whether technological advance does and can guarantee real progress. If man when he lives on the moon is the same type of man we know now, it will only be the story of earth all over again. Only if the space-man of the future is governed by intelligence, honour and beauty, to cite Bernard Shaw's trio, only if love and compassion reign, could it be said that human existence on other planets than earth could be either desirable or tolerable. Even in outer space, individuals would still die. Or do we wish to maintain seriously the possibility of immortality in the present body? Some today are toying with such ideas as discovering the secret of renewing cells which might extend the individual life indefinitely, or perhaps one day defeat death itself. In view of the fantastic ideas floating around today and when the remarkable possibilities of transplants of organs are taken into account, the sober conclusion of a modern medical expert is worth bearing in mind. 'Under normal circumstances a person is as dead today as he was a thousand years ago if his heart does not beat for five minutes.'[1]

Yet the basic issue would remain even if we manage to live to three hundred years like the earlier biblical figures, or the elders of Shaw's dramatic fantasy. Can a viable theology of hope really be built upon the possibility of defeating death by technological skill? If the answer to this is in the negative, then the problem takes the form: Is it possible to combine in one coherent theology a positive hope for man's future in this world and a confident anticipation of an eternal life beyond the present order of space and time? It has been notoriously difficult for Christians to maintain the proper balance between these two demands. It seems as if some kind of precarious equilibrium can only be preserved by allowing the pendulum to swing from one extreme to the other. In practice, however, this is no real solution. If we want the courage and patience to continue Christian activity in this world, we need the eternal hope to sustain us and free us from utopian fanaticism. If, on the other hand, we are already convinced that man's final home is beyond this world, and that men are always sojourners and pilgrims in the world, we need to remind ourselves that God must have some reason for creating the world and keeping it in being as long as He has done. We have deliberately evaded such contemporary issues as pollution and the problems of ecology. If the earth is the Lord's, then it follows for the Christian in particular that man must take a responsible attitude towards the natural world and the way in which he uses its God-given resources.[2] This duty to keep the environment a clean and wholesome place in which to live does not eliminate the need of an answer to the question we have raised about the ultimate fate of the individual. Certainly, the Bible does encourage us to believe that the will of God can be done in earth as in heaven. Our task now will be to take another look at the Bible's view of man and his destiny and see if the insights there disclosed will enable us to achieve von Hugel's 'otherworldliness without fanaticism and this-worldliness without Philistinism.'

[1] A. Toynbee and others, *Man's Concern with Death*, p. 23.
[2] H. Montefiore, *Can Man Survive?*, p. 42.

Chapter Three

Theology Without Hope

The title of this present chapter is obviously ambiguous. It could also have been called 'A study in radical this-worldliness'. There seems to be some merit at this early stage of our investigation in considering the case of a modern Christian thinker for whom this question of an after-life is not of the heart of the matter. If a convincing theology can be developed without the assumption that men survive death, then wisdom would dictate that the discussion of this question should be left to those who are interested in such esoteric topics. In any full-scale treatment of the Christian faith, it would occupy a very peripheral place indeed. The phrase 'theology of hope' is already being used as if it connoted a 'school' of Christian thinkers, all sharing the same perspective. It would, however, obviously be unfair to compile a list of such men as Moltmann, Pannenberg, Braaten, Metz, Cox and others as if their hope for man's future on this earth necessarily excluded the hope of personal immortality. That this latter belief does occupy a very peripheral role in the thought of many Christian thinkers today could, I believe, be shown. This would apply to some who are not generally associated with the 'theology of hope' as well as to some who are. The very phrase 'Theology of hope' may give a wrong impression to the uninitiated. One might think that previous generations of Christians have not known what true Christian hope is, and that it has been left to the twentieth century to discover it. But how do we classify those who come within this category? Were Barth and Tillich theologians of hope, and if not, why not? What about Bonhoeffer? Is Langdon Gilkey today not a theologian of hope? Or the late Austin Farrer of England? What qualifies a man to be so called? The one thing that most Christian thinkers of today have in common is an intense preoccupation with the future of man, and by future here is generally meant his future on earth. The reasons for this are obvious—nuclear power, the decline of any simple belief in inevitable progress, the question marks which hang over our immediate future. We are all deeply concerned about what is going to happen to us, not in the distant future, not in the after-life, but in the next few years. How can we overcome the despair which paralyses effective action? Now I have no doubt in my own mind that this is a most serious and urgent matter and Christians of all people cannot evade it. Nevertheless, in the midst of this preoccupation with our immediate earthly future, we are in grave danger of losing altogether another dimension of the Christian faith which speaks of the destiny of the individual, not only in this life, but beyond it. In this properly understood sense, I believe that there is an element of radical other-worldliness in the Christian faith which no jibe from humanist or Marxist about 'pie in the sky' ought to cause us to neglect. By other-worldliness, I do not mean the neglect of this world in which God has placed us, but the conviction that this world is not the only world there is. How could it be if God is as Christians believe Him to be? It ought to be possible to combine a positive hope for this world, for man's future on this planet, without evading the problem of death and the ultimate destiny of the individual person. We do not have to choose between the 'God ahead of us' and the 'God above us'. A complete Christian faith can have both.

I would like to develop my own point of view by a critical assessment of some sections of Gordon Kaufman's *Systematic Theology: A Historicist Perspective*.[1] Since my remarks are going to be mainly critical, I would hasten to add that there is much in this book which is splendidly biblical and profoundly true. Indeed, until I arrived at the final sections I was frequently uttering a grateful amen. It is delightfully written, intellectually honest and courageous in its determination to remain true to certain fundamental biblical insights. It is not impressionist and off the cuff as some of the pronouncements of the radical theologians tend to be. It is not superficially humanist or iconoclastic in regard to the Christian tradition. It is solid, serious, well-argued and for that very reason, all the more dangerous, at least on the questions with which I am concerned in this paper. It is not my intention, as I have indicated, to discuss here every aspect of the thesis developed in this book, but only to indicate its bearings upon our special interest at the moment, namely the nature of Christian hope in relation to personal survival after death. Since it would be tedious to give detailed quotations in justification of every comment made, I would urge you to study Professor Kaufman's book and particularly chapters 27–30. This will enable you to check what is here said against the author's statements and assess the validity of the interpretation

[1] G. Kaufman, *Systematic Theology: A Historicist Perspective*.

here given. It is only in these later chapters that it becomes clear where Dr Kaufman is leading us. Let me begin with a provocative statement and see how far it can be justified. It would seem that this book develops its doctrine of God on the basis of early Hebrew thought before belief in an after-life worth the having became characteristic of one important strand of later Judaism. It is well known to biblical scholars that the early Hebrews affirmed their belief in the living, holy, righteous and transcendent God without feeling the need at this stage of their history to deduce from this any doctrine of resurrection or personal immortality. Sheol was the abode of the shades, an unreal existence which inspired no hope and from which the pious Israelite prayed to be delivered. The 'Day of the Lord', the hope of a future reign of God, Messianic expectations, all had to do with a future existence on this earth, not translation to a transcendent realm beyond space and time. This was obviously not true of later Judaism nor, I would say, of early Christian faith itself, but it is the early Hebrew position which appeals to Professor Kaufman. If the purpose of God is to be manifested, vindicated and fulfilled, it must be in terms of the historical existence man knows in this world. One might also observe that the author has a point of contact with the kind of hope that has inspired various forms of millennialism. It is a very sophisticated version which is offered to us, since Kaufman is not committed to any literal interpretation of the images and symbols of traditional millennialism, but he does share its basic hope of a reign of God under the conditions of historical existence. 'The ultimate arbiter of theological validity is not reason or experience or the Bible or the church but the movement of history itself—understood theologically: the providence of God.'[1]

It is a help to the understanding of chapters 27–30 to remember the statement there found: 'For individuals die in a matter of a few years and we have no reason to suppose that their life continues beyond the grave.'[2] This statement is justified on a number of different grounds. First the Hebrew psychology of the whole man, in which man is inseparable from his body, precludes any survival of personality without the body. Since the physical body cannot survive death, therefore persons cannot survive death. This presumably is further confirmed by modern biological and psychological views of the psychosomatic unity of man. The author does not attempt from this starting-point to rehabilitate some doctrine of resurrection, but prefers to affirm that

[1] G. Kaufman, *Systematic Theology: A Historicist Perspective*, p. xv.
[2] ibid., p. 464.

man's psychosomatic unity is inseparably bound to its physical base and that, therefore, life after death in any sense is not possible. This presupposition is obviously of major importance for the author's treatment of the resurrection of Jesus, not to mention our own survival of death. We do not need to examine now the details of his treatment of the historical evidence, though this would be required to give a fully reasoned answer to the view adopted. Our concern here is to get clear exactly what is being said. The author is convinced on historical grounds that the story of the empty tomb is a legend. It is understandable that the early disciples were attracted by such an additional confirmation in physical fact of the mysterious experiences which are known as the resurrection appearances. We do not need to accuse the disciples of inventing the story for dishonest purposes. It was a natural deduction, but it remains the case that it has no basis in fact. Whatever we say about the resurrection of Jesus, therefore, must concentrate exclusively upon the Pauline account. Paul, it is stressed, does not specifically mention the empty tomb, nor are we justified in deducing anything from the fact that he insists that Jesus was buried, unless it be the reality of the death which no one has ever questioned. The problem, therefore, concerns the nature of the appearances. We need not now debate the propriety of attaching the description 'hallucinations' to the appearances, though, as the author admits, it suggests to the average person an abnormal psychological experience which is not grounded in any reality 'outside' the psychic experience of the individual. The word 'hallucination' is defended, however, on the grounds that 'it points to such a nonpublic but privately extremely significant experience. It is a type of experience moreover which not infrequently accompanies genuine creativity.[1] In so far as the word hallucination tends to remind Christians that their faith is a scandal and an absurdity, that is all to the good.

What, then is the proper interpretation of these hallucinations in which the early disciples thought they saw 'Jesus'? Professor Kaufman does not try to interpret them as veridical mystical visions with ontological import, in other words that in these visions the disciples were assured of the present and living reality of their Lord on the other side of death. This cannot be the true interpretation because dead men do not live again after death as individual persons, with or without a body of any kind. Traditional Christian belief was mistaken in thinking of a personal continuity of Jesus between His life on earth and His life in the resurrection mode. The important thing for us is

[1] G. Kaufman, *Systematic Theology: A Historicist Perspective*, p. 425.

'not that this finite man as such lives again, but that God's act begun in him was a genuine historical act which still continues.[1] This, however, was an act which continues, not in a realm beyond death but in a historical process of transformation which continues now in this world. Obviously there is no truth on this basis in the classical Christian view that the risen Christ took back to the Father our glorified humanity and thus became the guarantor of our survival as persons. We have already been told that dead men do not live again after death. What was creative and new in the resurrection appearances (or hallucinations) was not the transition of the risen Christ to an existence beyond death, but the breaking of God's presence into history and the continuing effects of this to the present day and the fact that it points to a future historical fulfilment of God's purpose in this world. 'Contemporary belief', he assures us, 'will not necessarily involve the conviction that the crucified Jesus became personally alive again.'[2] He also goes on to make the somewhat astonishing remark that it was a good thing that the 'appearances' or 'hallucinations' took place when they did nearly two thousand years ago or 'modern times would hardly be propitious for such a momentous event.'[3] The implication seems plainly to be that, if Christianity had originated today it would never have got off the ground, because it could never have generated the faith and confidence required for its historical survival in our more sophisticated society.

It is only fair to Professor Kaufman to observe that he does not claim that the view he is advocating really reflects the mind of the early Church. 'Although it cannot be denied that the view I am taking here is different from that of any of the biblical writers,[4] he says, he is comforted by the thought that it is very near to the position adopted by the apostle Paul. This again is a large assumption that requires a good deal of substantiating, but let us leave it there for the moment. It is rather curious that in his discussion of the resurrection appearances or hallucinations, he replies to possible objectors: 'Or can God not speak and act through visions and voices? If one took such a position he would in his modernity be discrediting such testimony both in the Bible and out, moreover, he would be putting very questionable restrictions on God Himself.'[5] This seems odd, for some will feel that Professor Kaufman is himself putting precisely such questionable restrictions upon God. How is he so confident that dead men do not

---

[1] G. Kaufman, *Systematic Theology: A Historicist Perspective*, p. 429.
[2] ibid., p. 426.   [3] ibid., p. 426.
[4] ibid., p. 430.   [5] ibid., p. 425.

live again, or that God could not raise Jesus Christ to a continued existence beyond death? It can only be that he is so persuaded of the negative answer to these questions because modern knowledge (science, philosophy, historical investigation, etc.) make a positive answer impossible. Yet these basic presuppositions, derived as he believes from modern thought, are never clearly exhibited and brought out into the light of day. Why are 'hallucinations' not subject to the same radical scepticism as the rest of the evidence? Indeed, is it more plausible to deny that God could not raise Jesus from the dead and then argue that God can speak through 'hallucinations'? In asking whether God cannot speak through hallucinations, visions, etc., he might well have considered a point made years ago by Professor A. E. Taylor that if God can bend psychological law to His purpose, why not physical law? On what grounds do we assert that God can break through the determinism of psychological law and not that of physical law? One could argue for a consistent determinism which would put both psychological and physical law beyond the power of God to modify. In that case, Kaufman cannot appeal to his hallucinations any more convincingly than the orthodox believer will appeal to the empty tomb. On the other hand, if rigid determinism is itself subjected to radical criticism, then the arguments against Jesus' existence after death are no longer so compelling. If one believes in God at all in the biblical sense, are we justified in putting upon Him, to use Professor Kaufman's phrase, such questionable restrictions? Of course, this whole discussion involves that we know exactly what the limits of natural law are, and therefore what God cannot do. This is a subject, however, which deserves far more adequate treatment than has been given to it.[1]

Let us try to summarize the results of this kind of approach to the renewal of faith and hope in Christian theology in our generation. Unlike the 'God is dead' advocates, Kaufman seems to be saying that we can still believe in the living and transcendent God such as characterized early Hebrew religion, a God who is working out a purpose which is to be fulfilled in a realm of God established on this earth and, therefore, under conditions of space and time. Since dead men do not live again, not even Jesus Christ Himself, then there are millions of human beings who have lived, suffered, and died who will not share in the future kingdom on earth. Jesus, of course, will not be there except in so far as His influence has permeated and transfigured the

[1] N. Smart, *Philosophers and Religious Truth*. The discussion in this book on Miracles and Hume is very relevant to this whole question.

existence of men through a long process of historical development. As far as I can discover, Kaufman does not discuss the question as to whether he believes that the present cosmos will always be such as to sustain human life or whether this earthly kingdom can be permanent.

Now the interesting thing is that this view is put forward as a Christian view of the matter. It is clear that if this is the case, then the term Christian must be allowed to have a much wider connotation than has been the case in the past. That the main stream of Christian belief has included such items as the resurrection of Jesus Christ to a continued existence beyond death and the survival of death by the believer does not count decisively in his view. We are free to modify and select. The vital question is as to how far this process of modification can go without the end result being startlingly different from the 'historic' faith. When does the reinterpretation of the gospel become no longer Christian in an intelligible and consistent sense and in a manner which requires a drastic departure from the New Testament witness? Professor Kaufman is not alone in thinking as he does about this question of life after death. Dr Schubert Ogden, in a very penetrating essay on 'The Promise of Faith' leaves us in no doubt as to where he stands. 'But what I must refuse to accept, precisely as a Christian theologian, is that belief in our subjective existence after death is in some way a necessary article of Christian belief.'[1] He is honest enough to admit that his 'promise of faith' leaves completely open 'whether we somehow manage to survive death and continue to exist as experiencing subjects as is claimed by conventional theories of immortality.[2] There would be nothing surprising and unexpected to find this being said by a humanist, an agnostic, a Marxist, or even a certain kind of absolute idealist, to name only a few. What is provocative is the claim that this attitude to personal survival can be properly designated Christian. It must be remembered in justice to Kaufman that he expressly repudiates a humanist solution to the questions raised by man's destiny in history. If the rule of love, righteousness and justice is ever established under historical conditions of space and time, it will be the work of God. Man is not a passive instrument in this process. He is a responsible covenant-partner with God, and God will not secure the triumph of His purpose without the creative action of grace and love which can bring about the transformation of man from inside without his destruction as a person.

[1] S. Ogden, *The Reality of God and Other Essays*, p. 230.
[2] ibid., p. 229.

With this we are in hearty agreement against the economic determinism of a Marx or the liberal humanism which anchors man's future solely and exclusively in man's own hands. But Professor Kaufman has, in fact, put all his eggs in one basket. His hopes depend on some future historical realization and if for any reason this fails, then there is nowhere else he can turn. Whatever may be said about God, there is only this present world as far as men are concerned.

What we have now to consider, however, is whether such a position offers a viable basis for hope, and for the Christian hope in particular. For me, it is essentially a theology without hope. It could no doubt be argued that since the reality of God is preserved, hope can remain, for after all Christian hope is in the last analysis confidence in God. The fact that death is the end for me as an individual person, and also for any earthly fulfilment of the kingdom, does not alter the fact that God remains. What is of value in me or in the historical process as a whole will be preserved in God, even though all men, Jesus included, will pass for ever from conscious life and existence. It is not to be denied that a plausible case can be made in general terms for such a view. Such a faith could sustain men in a vigorous and positive activity under historical conditions, as early Hebrew Yahwism proves. Yet there remains more than a lurking doubt whether such a faith can bear the full weight of man's conscious awareness of his finitude and ultimate death. Later developments in Judaism itself and in Christianity suggest that it cannot. The problem becomes more acute the more we try to defend a Christian view of the significance and worth of the human person. The more we insist that God is agape-love and that we are His children, the more irreconcilable becomes the notion of a divine parent who is content to let the millions of His children perish, content only to remember that He once had them. This is not because of our ingrained sentimentality or basic selfishness. It is an inescapable consequence of the affirmation that God is love. It puts a strain almost impossible to bear upon a faith which believes that the 'blood, toil, tears and sweat' of the human story ends, as it began, with God divested of His children and existing in splendid isolation. Kaufman rightly says that we could never call God 'Father' with confidence on the basis of a scientific knowledge of nature. Only the Christ-event can give us this confidence and trust.[1] Furthermore, even the Christ-event could not give us this confidence if it were only a past historical event uninterpreted by God's present activity through the Holy Spirit in man's contemporary experience. All this is splendidly true,

[1] G. Kaufman, op. cit., p. 245.

but instead of accepting the full consequences of the spiritual logic involved in calling God Father on the basis of the Christ-event, even Jesus Himself is consigned to ultimate oblivion, along with all who have confessed Him and trusted in Him and His promises.

It is our judgement that this is not an adequate basis for Christian hope. The ambiguities in Kaufman's discussion on pp. 470–4 are indeed confusing. It seems to be clearly asserted that man must be content to serve God while fully accepting his finite creaturely nature and the death which is the divinely determined end of such existence. 'There is no reason whatsoever to suppose that an everlasting extension of his finite existence would somehow be a great and glorious consummation for human life.[1] This, however, as we have said, is ambiguous. Christians are not committed to believe that man's finite existence continues in exactly the same form as now. This is denied both by Jesus and Paul. Paul Tillich's comment, quoted with approval by Kaufman, that 'an infinity of the finite could be a symbol for hell'[2] rests on the same ambiguity. Mere duration in itself, mere going on and on, could be a hell, but then the doctrine of the resurrection of the whole man was never intended to suggest mere duration apart from the lived experience of abundant life which is possible in Christ. One might argue with equal logic that life in Christ now would be boring and hell if it lasted too long. Kaufman never seems to have considered the possibility of a personal existence after death which could be meaningful and significant because it is 'in Christ' and therefore a perpetual vehicle for the presence and activity of God and the occasion for the unending and exciting expression of new creative possibilities as God's eternal covenant-partner. It is admitted that man has to have some 'image' of a fulfilment to sustain his energy and his hope. For Kaufman, this is a future historical realization that shows God to be the Lord of history. On the basis, however, of his denial of personal survival in any sense, this means that countless millions are not going to have any conscious share in the ultimate consummation. Their reward is to know that they have contributed in some measure to it. Yet even our author seems to admit that man may need something more than this. The symbols of heaven and hell, he tells us, of salvation and judgement at the 'end', point to the fact that every historical decision and action taken by men with respect to God's revelation is not of mere ephemeral or passing import.[3] 'Their consequences', he goes on, 'will be felt through the entire future indeed through all

[1] G. Kaufman, op. cit., p. 470.
[2] ibid., p. 470.   [3] ibid., p. 472.

eternity.'[1] What does this latter phrase mean? Not, as we have made abundantly clear, an eternity of personal existence, an everlasting communion of saints beyond space and time as we know them. It can only mean that God remembers them and preserves them and their significance in His memory. Yet there are real difficulties in this suggestion. There is, after all, a vast difference between a parent having memories of his child and seeing the child grow up and mature to a point where father and son can delight in their mutual fellowship. There is a great difference between my hoping that God will remember me and believing that I shall one day enjoy a fellowship with Him which death cannot destroy. There are also more abstruse theological and philosophical difficulties. If Kaufman or someone else were to press too far their objections to a too literal use of the symbols men use to point to God, if, for example, consciousness and memory are regarded as too anthropomorphic to apply to God, then we would end up, not only with the death of all men but even with a God who did not remember His children and their heroic decisions of faith, trust and obedience while here on earth. One can imagine a certain kind of Hindu or Buddhist speaking like this. It seems odd to offer this as a basis for Christian hope.

Our conclusion, then, is that this solution is inadequate and insufficient. The root of the difficulty lies in the way Kaufman understands the Christ-event and in the nature of his biblical exegesis. If he did not feel compelled to interpret Scripture in a manner significantly different from that of the New Testament witnesses themselves, and this he does on his own admission, then the resulting position would be vastly different. It is frequently said, and constantly repeated, that to believe in heaven is to take men's minds away from the pressing problems of earth and induce a social indifference or passive acceptance of the status quo with all its suffering and injustice. Marx said this, and many who are not Marxists have swallowed his critique of religion and of Christianity in particular without subjecting it to critical examination. Let us admit that some Christians in the past, and indeed today, have failed to hold the proper balance between earth and heaven. There is, however, another side to the story. Not all Christians have used their hope of heaven as an excuse to evade the pressing issues of this world. Rather it has given them the faith and courage to persist in the face of opposition, hostility, misunderstanding and the threat of violent death. Let us not blink at the facts. The many who have died and sacrificed for the Marxist Utopia will never survive to

[1] G. Kaufman, op. cit., p. 472.

live in it. The same is also true for Kaufman's future reign of God on earth, for there is no resurrection of believers who die before this comes about. It is sentimentality to say that we should be satisfied to live in our descendants, for they too face death. The Christian hope, on the other hand, has a word to speak about the individual person and his destiny. If he perishes, so does the race. If in this life only we have hope in Christ, we are of all men most to be pitied. I do not know whether many people read today the work of Baron von Hügel, a prominent Roman Catholic layman in England at the turn of the century. He has many wise things to say which we would do well to heed. I end with his declaration that the Christian must aim at 'otherworldliness without fanaticism and thisworldliness without Philistinism'. We are citizens of two worlds—of this world where God has placed us to do His will and of that city with firm foundations, whose architect and builder is God. (Heb. 11:10)

Chapter Four

What Did Jesus Have to Say?

Having criticized the exclusive this-worldly orientation of some modern thinkers, we shall now turn to a discussion of what Jesus had to say on this subject. The non-Christian will no doubt always be baffled by this kind of appeal. Suffice it to say now that we are asking quite specifically whether the Christian faith has anything to say about this problem of death and man's survival of it. It is no use debating whether Christian ideas are valid or not until we have satisfied ourselves that it is saying something relevant and pertinent on this question. There seems no need now to go over again the biblical material. The standard works are there for all to consult. They have been usefully summarized in David Edwards's *The Last Things Now*.[1] As far as we are concerned, we accept the conclusion of Old Testament scholarship that any positive conception of a life after death worth having was a late development in Judaism. It does not dominate the literature of the Old Testament as we have it. For this we must go to the writings between the testaments. This, however, does not solve our problem. For the Christian, his theology of death will be determined by the New Testament and the light shed upon this issue by Jesus Christ. Even in regard to the Old Testament itself, it is necessary to ask whether all the developments of later Judaism were a mistaken deviation or whether some of them were legitimate developments from Old Testament insights. Professor H. D. Lewis has doubts about excluding the personal hope, even within the Old Testament history proper. 'Even where the more explicit emphasis is on the eventual destiny of the nation in this world, I find it hard to account for all the expressions of hope and of divine concern for man in the Bible without reference to an expectation, throughout the history which the Bible reflects, of personal as well as collective salvation.'[2] Be this as it may, a Christian must inevitably ask what Jesus had to say about this question, for He is his ultimate authority in matters of faith.

[1] D. L. Edwards, *The Last Things Now*.
[2] H. D. Lewis, *Philosophy of Religion*, p. 317.

It is not our intention to discuss here on what grounds and by what right a Christian asks the authority of Christ. This would require a full study of the doctrine of Christ and indeed of the philosophy of religion too. We simply start from the assumption that, historically speaking, Christians are those who confess that Jesus is Lord and therefore accept His authority. A Christian will, therefore, instinctively ask himself what Jesus had to say on a certain matter before reaching his own personal conclusions. It is obvious that this may involve him in complex matters of biblical interpretation. If he finally comes to the conclusion that the 'mind of Christ' completely eludes him, then no doubt, if he is logical, he will cease to be a Christian in the sense of accepting the final authority of Jesus Christ. All we are contending for at the moment is that the Christian will naturally ask the question, 'What did Jesus say?' when such a matter as personal immortality is raised.

It is true that Jesus does not have much to say when judged quantitatively in terms of the number of words used. This, however, surely does not entitle us to ignore what He does say or play down its importance. Nor need we debate in detail here the more radical applications of the form-critical method which would leave us in complete doubt as to whether we can ever be sure of anything Jesus thought or said. If this position were substantiated, then it goes without saying that we could not speak of Jesus' attitude to death or personal survival, only of what the early Christian communities thought He said. We certainly have Mark 12: 18 ff. Bultmann says of it: 'So the debate in 12: 18–25 simply reflects the theological activity of the Church.'[1] There is something irritatingly indefinite about this kind of comment. What are we supposed to deduce from it? That the Church's theological activity was not in any way prompted by anything that Jesus said. But how does Bultmann know this? It should be added that in his *Theology of the New Testament*, Bultmann does say that 'He [i.e. Jesus] expects the resurrection of the dead (Mark 12: 18–27) and the judgment (Luke 11: 31 ff.)' without suggesting any real doubt about the ascription to Jesus of this way of thinking.[2] Vincent Taylor, on the other hand, thinks that 'genuine tradition of the most primitive kind' is preserved in this passage and that 'unobtrusive but clearly discernible, are the moral elevation of Jesus, the spirituality of His outlook and the force of His personality.'[3] The

[1] R. Bultmann, *The History of the Synoptic Tradition*, tr. John Marsh, p. 26.
[2] R. Bultmann, *Theology of the New Testament*, vol. i, p. 6.
[3] V. Taylor, *The Gospel according to St Mark*, p. 480.

passage in question concerns the familiar case of the woman who married seven brothers in succession. In reply to the question of the Sadducees as to whose wife she would be in the resurrection, Jesus replies: 'You are mistaken, and surely this is the reason: you do not know either the scriptures or the power of God. When they rise from the dead, men and women do not marry; they are like angels in heaven.' (Mark 12: 24–5. N.E.B.) We do not need to deny that this incident reflects the debate in late Judaism and in the early Christian communities between the Pharisees and the Sadducees concerning both the reality and the nature of the resurrection. Christopher Evans is of the opinion that the doctrine of the resurrection was not such as could be taken for granted in the Judaism of Jesus' day. He thinks it was not firmly fixed in the Jewish tradition of the time.[1] This may be admitted without conceding that later Judaism made no contribution in this area. After all, it was a strand in late Jewish thought of not negligible importance, and Jesus thought it worth while to take it up and make it the vehicle for His own reflections. This in no way contradicts the main point which Evans seems concerned to make, namely that any adequate doctrine of resurrection in the Christian sense must depend mainly upon the resurrection of Jesus Himself.

The reply of Jesus certainly seems to suggest that the mode of the resurrection life will differ considerably from life in the present body. The fact that men and women do not marry in this new existence also implies the superfluous nature of some of the physical organs which we now possess. It strongly implies a resurrection body which is not an exact duplicate of our present one. This kind of language is not peculiar to Jesus. For example, in 1 Enoch 109: 4 we have: 'Ye shall have great joy as angels of heaven' and in the Apocalypse of Baruch: 'the righteous shall be made like unto the angels, and be made equal to the stars'. (51: 10) Even more striking is the quotation by Taylor from Berakoth 17a of Rab, a Babylonian teacher: 'in the life to come there is no eating and drinking, no begetting of children, no bargaining, jealousy, hatred and strife but that the righteous sit with crowns on their heads and are satisfied with the glory of God.'[2]

If, on the other hand, we assume with Bultmann that the reply is not from Jesus but a reflection of a debate going on in the early Church on this matter, then some unknown Christian came up with this rather penetrating reply, and its truth or not would still have to be judged on its merits. The Markan account then quotes Jesus as

[1] C. F. Evans, *Resurrection and the New Testament*. Studies in Biblical Theology, Second Series 12, pp. 31, 39. [2] Taylor, op. cit., p. 483.

recalling to them the story of the burning bush and how God said to Moses: 'I am the God of Abraham, the God of Isaac, and the God of Jacob. God is not God of the dead but of the living.' (Mark 12: 27–7. N.E.B.) Taken quite out of context, this could be given a Sadducean interpretation, but this seems very unlikely. Dr Nineham quotes Wellhausen's remark that the Old Testament drew from the bush passage the opposite conclusion to that which Jesus seems to be drawing here, namely that because God is the God of the living, therefore the dead are excluded from all living and meaningful relationship to Him.[1] It seems very improbable that this is the meaning in this context. Jesus appears to be asserting God's power in the realm of the so-called dead, and furthermore implying that they continue to live as recognizable and distinct persons. There is here no hint of absorption or of the swallowing up of individuality. It is true that the passage taken alone might only point to life after death and not necessarily to a specific doctrine of resurrection. For many Christians, these words of Jesus have been a sufficient basis for their conviction that the Christian survives death as a distinct person in a more glorious mode of existence called the 'resurrection of the body' without this involving the resuscitation of the unchanged physical body which we now have. It would be difficult to deduce from this Markan passage that Jesus was only speaking of a new quality of life here and now. This does not mean that He rejected this idea, for there is plenty of evidence that He conceived the entry into the kingdom, or the coming under the rule of God, as involving a radical transformation of the character of the disciple in this life. Nevertheless, Mark 12: 18 ff. does seem to speak clearly of a life after death, and this is the point we are concerned with now.

If, however, the passage stood entirely alone, we might regard it as an exception which in this case does not prove the rule. It would then be regarded as out of harmony with Jesus' otherwise exclusive concern with the rule of God on earth under historical conditions. It is not altogether clear where David Edwards stands on this issue. He remarks that we do not share the attitude of the Sadducees to the burning bush.[2] Presumably this means that 'we' (i.e. modern men or some modern men) do not regard this as a theophany which gives us any reliable information about the reality or character of God. He also tells us that many modern people would agree with the Sadducees in their denial of any resurrection.[3] This is true as a statement of fact

[1] D. E. Nineham, *St Mark*, Pelican Commentary, p. 322.
[2] D. L. Edwards, *The Last Things Now*, p. 64.   [3] ibid., p. 65.

about some people then and now. It does not prove that they were right. This question must be discussed later on its merits. The same author, discussing the theological concepts which link death with Adam's sin, admits that out of the biblical witness, despite our doubts about such ideas as the above, the conviction arises that 'death is not the proper end for the person whom God loves'. What exactly does this mean? One might assume that if it is not the proper end, then some other end is proper and that is the survival of bodily death. It is not clear however that this is what he means. 'We can', he says, 'pay a tribute to this great biblical protest against death.'[1] What precisely is 'paying tribute' in this connection? We can, says Edwards, take it seriously, if not literally. But again, what does 'seriously' involve? Certainly, a protest against death is not the same as a settled conviction that death can be conquered and that man will survive it. The above writer is quite convinced that man's soul is not naturally immortal.[2] This will have to be considered as a separate issue later. Even if this is true it is still possible that the Bible might teach the power of God in enabling man to survive death, even if the soul, however conceived, is not intrinsically immortal.

Let us return for a moment to the exegesis of the passage in question. Not all are as sceptical as Bultmann about the incident as giving us at least some indication of Jesus' attitude to the question. In the commentary of Major, Manson and Wright entitled *The Mission and Message of Jesus*, Dr Major does not question the authenticity of the incident but comments that 'Jesus thus teaches, not only a doctrine of the future life, but one which is not dependent upon a materialistic doctrine of the resurrection as was the contemporary Pharisaic doctrine'.[3]

This seems to be the position adopted by Dr Nineham, who seems to accept Jesus' reply as a pronouncement going back to Him. He does not exclude the possibility that Jesus sometimes thought it right to fight His opponents with their own weapons, as in the case of the Sadducees. He also adds that from the point of view of the later Gentile church, Jesus' statement 'will have been of the greatest significance as suggesting a spiritual view of the resurrection, free from the crudely materialistic traits which we know to have been a genuine stumbling block to more spiritually minded Greeks'.[4]

We seem to be on reasonably firm ground therefore in asserting

---

[1] D. L. Edwards, *The Last Things Now*, p. 71.   [2] ibid., p. 71.
[3] H. D. A. Major, T. W. Manson, and C. J. Wright, *The Mission and Message of Jesus*, p. 150.   [4] Nineham, op. cit., p. 321.

that Jesus did make a pronouncement on this question of man's survival of death, however much this was embedded in our documents in situations reflecting later controversies in the early Church. If this is a reasonable conclusion, then we must give full weight to it in the context of Jesus' total message. If men do survive death, in whatever mode or existence, it must surely influence profoundly the total perspective from which one views the present life. It is unrealistic and psychologically improbable to say the least, that Jesus took his stand on this issue and then dismissed it from His mind as having no further significance. He must have had a hope in the resurrection in the sense in which He understood the phrase. It also appears that St Paul was basically in harmony with Jesus' thought on this issue when He develops His view of the 'spiritual body' and asserts that 'flesh and blood cannot inherit the kingdom of God'. Certainly Paul seems to affirm some kind of continuity between life in the body now and life in the resurrection body in the age to come. It is not however a resuscitation of the physical body unchanged and un-transformed. The conclusion to be drawn, then, is that both Jesus and Paul affirm man's survival of death in a new mode of resurrection life in which the 'person' will continue to exist in more than a sym-bolical sense. Whatever else is said about God's purposes for men on this earth, it seems quite contrary to the evidence to deny this dimension of an eternal existence for men in a realm beyond space and time. If this is an integral part of the teaching of Jesus, even before the resur-rection of Jesus itself, have we the right to produce our own version of the faith from which this element is lacking and continue to call the result 'Christianity'? If what has been said is justified, then why is it that the resurrection has been interpreted in influential strands of the Christian tradition as if it meant the retention of our present bodies and all their organs, even in the resurrection state when these organs will no longer have any direct use? The answer to this question is closely related to the resurrection of Jesus Himself and to the interpretation, influenced by Hebrew psychology, which makes the survival of a person without his present body both impossible and unattractive if it were. Christian confidence in our survival of death has of course depended not only upon statements such as those of Mark 12: 18 ff. but upon the fact of Jesus' resurrection. Even if Jesus had said nothing on this subject, the fact, if such it be, that He Himself had survived death would have afforded for Christians the strongest possible basis for their confidence. It is however important to dis-tinguish certain factors before we proceed to a further consideration of Jesus' resurrection. Even if it could be proved that Jesus did not speak of His own resurrection as an 'event' which was soon to follow His death, it could be possible that He accepted the belief in the general resurrection of the end of the age, and that He would share along with all the righteous in that resurrection. This would mean that His own resurrection would simply be an outstanding instance of what would be true for all the righteous. This would further imply that His resurrection has not yet taken place and that Jesus awaits the final consummation, like everyone else, for His entry into the fullness of the resurrection life. This raises the question then, as to whether Jesus expected His own resurrection prior to the end of the age, namely within a very short period after His death.

It could also be maintained that He did expect it in the near future, that He was in fact mistaken about the imminence of it, but that none the less Jesus' survival of death is certain because of the truth of the doctrine of the general resurrection. According to this view, the general resurrection could not be deduced from the fact of Jesus' own resurrection, but rather the reverse. It is because the general resurrection is certain on the basis of the character of God and His previous actions in history, that we can now be sure of the final resurrection of Jesus, even if the Easter 'event' is open to grave doubts and difficulties from the point of view of modern historical investigation, and what we now know about the biology and psychology of the human person. One must admit, however, that it would be rather odd to talk of the resurrection of Jesus as still future, awaiting the end of the age, in the light of the overwhelming New Testament evidence that this event has already taken place. Believers, along with Jesus Himself, would still be awaiting the resurrection at the end of the age. In this case, the certainty of victory over death is a hope awaiting confirmation at the end of history, not a certainty rooted in the present fact of Jesus' resurrection.

What, then, is to be said about the resurrection of Jesus? A limited number of options is open to us, and we shall list them in turn in order to make clear what are the basic issues at stake.

(1) All historians, including form-critics, who have devoted themselves to a historical study of the origins of the Christian faith, agree that the early disciples arrived by whatever means at the conviction that Jesus had survived and conquered death. However much we may debate as to what actually happened, there is no doubting that the Easter faith was the most potent factor in stimulating in the early Church both its sense of mission and its joyous con-

fidence in the ultimate victory of the divine purpose. Bultmann concedes this point and Kaufmann agrees that this was the faith of the early Church, even if we cannot interpret what happened in the same sense as they did. The debate, therefore, continues, not about the question whether 'something' happened but about what happened. Professor Willi Marxsen, for example, maintains that the only thing of which we can be sure is that certain disciples of Jesus believed that they had 'seen' Him after death. We may also reach a fair historical certainty about their description of these appearances. They also 'interpreted' these experiences as proof that Jesus had risen from the dead, namely that He had survived death and that He 'was seen' or let Himself be seen, or else appeared.[1] Of these things we can be historically certain. What we are not free to do, according to Marxsen, is to jump straight from these historical certainties to the conclusion that the disciples' interpretation was in fact correct, namely that in fact Jesus had risen from the dead. It was natural enough that they should use the category of resurrection for the interpretation of their experiences, in view of its wide use in apocalyptic and indeed in the history of religion. It does not follow that this is the only category or that we today must adopt it. Marxsen also stresses the fact that even if the empty tomb could be given a high degree of historical certainty (and he does not believe this to be the case), it does not of itself prove the reality of Jesus' survival of death. Furthermore, no individual in the primitive community ever claimed actually to have seen the resurrection as an event, that is, presumably saw the body emerging from the tomb in its resurrection glory. The conclusion Marxsen draws is that 'the raising of Jesus is not the fundamental datum of Christianity but rather the words and deeds of Jesus.'[2] 'Christian theology, therefore, cannot, and may not, on any account, start from Jesus' resurrection.'[3]

Obviously on this view, one cannot immediately deduce from the resurrection of Jesus important conclusions for the survival of men in general. One has first to justify the interpretative category used by the first disciples and show that this is the only and inevitable category for the proper evaluation of the 'appearances'. This, thinks Marxsen, can in fact never be done. One could only fall back upon authority or the inspired truth of the apocalyptic doctrine of the

[1] C. F. D. Moule, *The Significance of the Message of the Resurrection for Faith in Jesus Christ*, Studies in Biblical Theology, Second Series No. 8, p. 47.

[2] ibid., p. 48.

[3] ibid., p. 48.

general resurrection. The only other alternative would be to abandon any appeal to biblical sources and do the best we can with philosophical considerations of a Platonic or some other kind. On Marxsen's view, since Christianity must start with the words and deeds of Jesus, anything we can say about life after death will depend upon the truth of whatever Jesus *said* on the subject and not upon the fact of the resurrection taken as an independent starting-point.

(2) A second option would be to say that the early Christians all believed in the immortality of the soul and that it was, therefore, a perfectly natural assumption that Jesus would survive death. We only mention this because of our desire to list all possible points of view. Suffice it to say that biblical scholarship is almost unanimous in rejecting this view. The reasons given are that the Old Testament neither affirms nor assumes man's survival of death as a 'soul' separated from his body. Hebrew psychology and its understanding of man made this impossible. Furthermore, the New Testament, despite the fact that we have it in Greek, is basically Hebrew and Jewish in its conception of what constitutes a man. Therefore, no interpretation of the New Testament language of resurrection can make use of the Greek conception of immortality. Perhaps this position is not as clear-cut and self-evident as some would assume. We believe it to be substantially accurate as far as its analysis of Hebrew psychology is concerned and the influence of this upon New Testament thought. It is still however, an open question whether Jewish and Christian thought evolved in a direction which brought it nearer to Greek thought than many may care to admit. Nevertheless, we cannot assume intrinsic immortality of the soul, separable from the body, as a determinative element in the thought of Jesus or in the way in which His resurrection was understood in the early Christian communities. That the thought of Jesus and of the early Christian community was not directly influenced by these Greek conceptions does not alter the fact already noted that He had obviously departed quite radically from the idea of a resuscitation of the present physical body in its biological entirety, and that He could and did conceive of a mode of existence after death which was radically different from life in the present body. This only shows once again that it is a great over-simplification of a very complex issue to put it in the form 'either immortality (Greek) or resurrection (Jewish and early Christian)'. We shall have occasion to notice in a later chapter the view of Professor James Barr on notions of immortality in late Judaism.

(3) This brings us to the place of the empty tomb in the New

Testament tradition and later Christian belief. It is argued that the 'story' or the 'legend' or the 'myth' of the empty tomb can be eliminated on various grounds. Either it does not stand up under rigorous historical scrutiny or even if it did, it would still have to be rejected on the grounds that a scientific world-view makes it impossible that men should rise from the dead with their present physical bodies, whether unchanged or even in a transformed body. Bultmann rejects the empty tomb on both of the above grounds, and many who are not Bultmannians have done and still do the same. It is worth observing that those who adopt this position are compelled to move nearer to the Greek view in some form if they want to affirm either Jesus' survival of death or ours. Kaufmann has logic on his side, perhaps, in denying survival for any man, including Jesus, in the light of his radical and negative analysis of the New Testament. It seems, however, unfair to play off Hebrew against Greek in any simple fashion, if one is going to employ the notion of the continued existence of Jesus after death in a mode which does not involve the retention of the physical body in exactly the same form in which He possessed it while on earth. Professor John Hick has said that Jesus did include as an essential element the affirmation of life after death but that He did not indicate 'the mode of the after-life life-whether embodied or disembodied, and if embodied, in what kind of material.'[1] If this is the case, then it is hardly possible to attack the label Hebrew or Greek to the thought of Jesus in any simple sense. That He retained the language of resurrection did not commit Him to the idea of physical resuscitation, though it may involve some notion of an 'embodied' existence after death. But if this 'spiritual body' is radically different from the present body, then we have moved that much nearer to a doctrine of personal immortality. Some developments in Jewish apocalytic show that this is not impossible, even for a Jew.

The implication of this line of argument, however, seems to be extremely serious for any who wish to defend the fact and the significance of the empty tomb and its implication of a 'corporeal' resurrection. If men can survive death without the present physical body, and this includes Jesus too, could He not have done so without His tomb being empty or His body disappearing from it without being subject to the normal and natural process of corruption? On this view, the appearances of the risen Lord were not dependent in any way upon the continuance of his physical body. After the crucifixion, Jesus could have passed to a new existence in the appro-

[1] J. Hick, *Christianity at the Centre*, p. 108.

priate spiritual body. The appearances would then be accounted veridical visions, whereby the disciples were assured of this continued existence after death.

Nevertheless, it has to be remembered that there is a big difference between a mystical vision interpreted as confirmation that Jesus was still alive and the conviction that they had actually encountered Jesus as alive after His death. This involves the view not only that Jesus was still alive after death but in some mysterious way He had passed through the barrier which at present separates the living and the dead, and had made Himself known again on this side of death. It is this conviction which distinguishes the resurrection of Jesus from a simple affirmation that He still lives after death, whether in an embodied or a disembodied form. It is the fact that He communicated with this side from the other side which raises such awkward questions for the contemporary mind influenced by the scientific outlook. A good illustration of this is Tillich's 'restitution' theory of the resurrection.[1] Having eliminated the empty tomb and any role of the physical body in the event of the resurrection, he is compelled to find some possible account of the Easter faith. He finds this in an ecstatic revelatory experience of the disciples in the light of which they come to the conviction that the 'new being', manifested most clearly in the total sacrifice of the Cross, could not be subject to death. They, therefore, applied to the Jesus who had died the symbol of resurrection which they had inherited from post-exilic Judaism. George Tavard has no difficulty in showing that this view finds little support in the exegesis of the New Testament.[2] Tavard exposes himself to criticism, however, in seeking to deduce the necessity of the 'bodily' resurrection from the Chalcedonian dogma and in speaking of Jesus as raising Himself. This is rare in the New Testament which usually speaks of God raising Jesus from the dead. Tavard would be in a stronger position if he had contented himself with appealing to the scriptural witness rather than making his position depend upon the Chalcedonian dogma. After all, it is not the resurrection of Jesus which gains its reality and significance from Chalcedon, but the latter which gains whatever validity it possesses from its ability to give an adequate account of the facts made known to us through the scriptural witness.

It could, of course be argued that the communication of the dead with the living is not a problem only in the case of the resurrection of

[1] P. Tillich, *Systematic Theology*, vol. ii, pp. 153 ff.
[2] G. H. Tavard, *Paul Tillich and the Christian Message*, pp. 113 ff.

Jesus. The spiritualist would contend that it has happened many times before and is still happening. In this case, the coming back of Jesus to communicate with his still living disciples was unusual but not exceptional. To reason in this way, however, demands that we already agree with the interpretation put by spiritualists and some psychical researchers upon certain phenomena connected with mediums and the like. If this evidence was widespread, clear and unambiguous and commanded the agreement of the great body of scientific men as to its proper interpretation, it would be possible to reason in this way. Failing this—with the resultant agnosticism in regard to psychical phenomena—then we have no option but to consider the resurrection of Jesus as not only unusual but one of a kind, altogether unique and without parallel. But, then, the evidence must be very compelling to justify us in accepting the disciples' interpretation of their experiences as not merely one possible interpretation (Marxsen), but as the only proper and normative interpretation of those experiences.

It is often assumed as self-evident that our entry into resurrection life, whether at death or the end of the age, must be of exactly the same kind as that of Jesus. Yet this is to beg many questions. Because Jesus came back to communicate with His disciples, it does not follow that when we die, we shall be able to move freely between this world and the next. The evidence is not very strong that this has in fact been the case with those who have already died in Christ. The 'appearances' of Christ could have served a special divine purpose integrally bound up with the vindication of Jesus, the confirmation and strengthening of the disciples' faith, and the creation of the Church as the body of Christ in the world. In this case His resurrection was more than the proof that a man can survive death. It was central to the total gospel of the reality of God's redeeming and triumphant love, even in the face of death, man's last enemy.

Could God have brought about this result by a series of appearances and visions which did not involve the empty tomb? Every Christian would hesitate about dogmatizing about what God could or could not do. The question resembles an earlier one as to whether God could have saved man apart from the death on the Cross, a question which everyone knows much occupied the mind of St Anselm in the twelfth century in *Cur Deus Homo*? There is no way in which such questions can be answered in the abstract. It is fruitless to ask whether God could have acted in some other way. The only fruitful method is to ask what is the evidence as to how in fact God has acted.

This brings us back to the New Testament and the biblical sources of our faith.

Having listed the various options, we shall now consider a more detailed study of their relative strength and weakness. At the risk of some repetition, we shall consider briefly the conclusions of Pannenberg in a recent study in which he grapples again with the question: in what sense, if any, was the resurrection of Jesus Christ a historical event? The following are his major points:

(*a*) There are two New Testament traditions concerning the appearances and the discovery of the empty tomb and these must be investigated separately.

(*b*) All the witnesses recognized Jesus of Nazareth in the appearances.

(*c*) There is good historical foundation for the view that the appearances of the risen Lord were really experienced by members of the primitive community.

(*d*) How, then, are the visions or appearances to be interpreted? Pannenberg comments: 'If by vision one understands a psychological event that is without a corresponding extrasubjective reality, then one can certainly not presuppose such a "subjective" concept of vision for the resurrection appearances as self-evident.'[1]

(*e*) Attempts since Strauss to explain the appearances in terms of mental and historical presuppositions on the part of the disciples have failed. We are justified, therefore, not only in talking of visions but of the appearances of the resurrected Jesus.

(*f*) We are not justified in denying this on the basis of a scientific view of natural laws which assumes without proof that we know what the limits of natural law are.

(*g*) Even if we did not have the tradition of the empty tomb, the evidence would still be strong that the disciples not only experienced subjective visions, but were really in contact with the risen Jesus after His death. In this sense, the resurrection is a historical event, because without it the reconstruction of the history cannot be made or intelligibly explained.

(*h*) Pannenberg believes that the tomb tradition and the appearance tradition came into existence independently of each other.[2] Nevertheless, the tomb tradition cannot be lightly dismissed and it is highly unlikely that the resurrection could have been effectively proclaimed in Jerusalem if the emptiness of the tomb had not been an acknowledged fact, even for the Jews.

[1] W. Pannenberg, *Jesus: God and Man*, p. 91.   [2] ibid., p. 105.

(i) The conclusion drawn is that the Easter faith is not faith divorced from historical considerations. 'As long as historiography does not begin with a narrow concept of reality according to which "dead men do not rise", it is not clear why historiography should not in principle be able to speak about Jesus' resurrection as the explanation that is best established of such events as the disciples' experiences of the appearances and the discovery of the empty tomb'.[1]

It is evident from this brief summary of Pannenberg's analysis of the New Testament material that he wishes to affirm the resurrection of Jesus Christ as a reality. It is not to be explained away only in terms of the subjective experiences of the disciples. Furthermore, it is a historical judgement because to assert the reality of the disciples' encounter with the risen Jesus is to make a statement about something which happened in historical events and without which these events cannot be made intelligible. It is also clear to Pannenberg that such a belief in the resurrection cannot be understood apart from the possession by the disciples of an interpretative principle which would enable them to make sense of the 'appearances'. This interpretative principle was already available to them in the apocalyptic hope of the future resurrection of the dead at the end of the age. This presupposition is not to be regarded as an aberration of late Judaism. It is the logical consequence of the Old Testament and the prophetic understanding of God and the inevitable and ultimate fulfilment of His purpose. To anyone who accepts the biblical faith in God, the later apocalyptic developments in the direction of a general resurrection must be accepted as valid. What, then, distinguishes the resurrection of Jesus is not merely the fact of resurrection itself. This was already a possible belief for the disciples and indeed for Jesus Himself, based upon their faith in the triumph of the divine purpose at the end of the age. This has some bearings upon the exegetical problems connected with those passages in the gospels where Jesus is shown as speaking of His own resurrection. For some it is incredible that He should have done so. I have heard it said that it is fantastic to believe that Jesus went to the cross in the conviction that He would be 'about again' in a few days. This is a superficial witticism, however, not worthy of the complexity of the problem. If Jesus believed in the general resurrection at the end of the age, as we have some reason to believe that He did, there is no reason at all to think that He could not have spoken of His own resurrection as God's final vindication of His purpose and of Jesus as the agent of that triumphant fulfilment. We do not have to assume

[1] W. Pannenberg, *Jesus: God and Man*, p. 109.

that Jesus in his earthly life had a detailed timetable of events in His mind. Indeed, He expressly disclaims such knowledge. That He was certain of His own resurrection as involved in His obedience to the will of the Father seems in no way unreasonable or impossible. This can be properly claimed without having to attribute to the earthly Jesus an omniscient awareness of every detail of the future.

The occasion for wonder is that, in the case of Jesus, His resurrection has already taken place before the end of the age, which is when one might have expected it to happen if general apocalyptic considerations were alone in view. The claim to authority by Jesus cannot, therefore, be based only on the words and ministry of Jesus as Marxsen suggests. The truth and validity of His claims were proleptic, that is they pointed forward to a future legitimation and confirmation and this was precisely what the resurrection of Jesus as a historical event provided. The disciples did not have to wait until the end of history to be sure of the final divine victory. The resurrection of Jesus before the end provided the basis of their confidence in the ultimate victory, despite the cross. One could never have deduced from the mere hope of the general resurrection the certainty that the sting of death had been removed. It would have remained a hope only. The disciples believed, rightly or wrongly, that the future hope was now securely anchored in the fact of Jesus' resurrection in the present aeon, in the present historical period in which all men now live. This took them a stage beyond either the apocalyptic hope of a general resurrection or a hope grounded in philosophical considerations of a Platonic sort.

It is clear, however, that much depends upon the validity of the apocalyptic hope of a general resurrection of the dead. If this could be disproved or rendered highly improbable, then the resurrection of Jesus itself would remain a sheer surd, an event completely detached from any intelligible context. But what arguments can be advanced in defence of the general hope of resurrection? It is obvious that no simple appeal can be made to the Old Testament since the doctrine of a general resurrection cannot be found in its pages. However, it could be argued, and I believe convincingly, that the Old Testament does supply us with an understanding of the nature and character of God in the light of which the apocalyptists were justified in drawing what deductions they did as to the general resurrection. This again is convincing provided one can accept the truth of the basic features of the Old Testament understanding of God. This, however, depends again not only upon certain historical events but upon a particular interpretation of these events, namely the prophetic. We are thus driven back to questions concerning the nature of the faith which inspired the prophetic interpretation of the events, and this in turn involves the validity of certain moral and spiritual perceptions and judgements.

The reasonableness of prophetic faith itself presupposes a certain metaphysic of values and the relationship of value-judgements to reality. Despite the modern distrust of metaphysics, there is no escaping from this conclusion. The reasonableness of the prophetic faith is not reconcilable with any metaphysic whatsoever. Nevertheless it presupposes a certain metaphysic, however inadequately articulated, if the prophetic faith is not simply accepted blindly but is put forward as reasonable, that is in accordance with the way things are or with the nature of reality. Prophetic faith cannot substantiate its claim to reasonableness in this sense in the total absence of any philosophical scheme of thought. Examples of the latter which I have in mind are indicated below.[1]

Pannenberg, however, is not content to defend the apocalyptic presupposition of the concept of general resurrection solely from the biblical concept of God. He also advances anthropological arguments which are of particular interest in the light of the contemporary emphasis upon human existence as limited exclusively to this world. He rightly insists in our view that, though man can only realize his humanity in community, no earthly society is totally adequate to this purpose. Such a view ignores the problem of death both for the living and for the dead, who are likewise cut off from ultimate fulfilment if death is really the end. A solidly based human hope demands a hope beyond death, and if this is denied, no satisfactory defence can be made of the final meaningfulness of our transient lives.[2] Impressive evidence can be collected for this position from the social sciences, anthropology, history, psychology and sociology. Here again, however, one cannot validly deduce from the problems of meaning created by death the certainty of a life beyond death apart from the certainty of Jesus' survival of death and a metaphysic of value. Nevertheless, a careful study of human existence in the face of death can provide powerful pointers in the direction of a faith and a philosophy which refuses to regard death as the final end. This is not to affirm that biblical faith is dependent upon philosophy construed as a set of principles or truths enunciated in detachment from the actual religious

[1] I. Trethowan, *Absolute Value*. J. B. Gibson, *Theism and Empiricism*. H. P. Owen, *The Christian Knowledge of God*.

[2] W. Pannenberg, *Jesus: God and Man,* pp. 84 ff.

experiences of men. It simply means that the full implications of biblical faith can only be made explicit in terms of some philosophy and that if the reasonableness of such faith is what one wishes to show, then the making of the implicit explicit is a requirement of thought.

Some will say that this means that the Christian believes in the reality of Jesus' resurrection on purely subjective grounds. This, however, is to beg the question. If a certain positivistic philosophy of science is valid, then no doubt it would be absurd to consider seriously the data to which the Christian appeals. Yet this is precisely the issue. While, therefore, it is true that the resurrection of Jesus cannot be deduced from a general philosophical principle, the fact remains that the very possibility of its not being merely wishful thinking depends also, not only upon the historical evidence as such, but upon general considerations concerning the nature of the world and man and the power on which they depend. The resurrection has to be asserted within the total context of belief in God, without which it could not possibly have the significance which Christians attribute to it. This means in effect that the Christian can have no interest in the resurrection in itself if he loses the battle about the reality and nature of God. In other words, the fact of Jesus' survival of death would become only an extraordinary phenomenon beyond the power of current science to explain. It would not necessarily have any religious significance.

How important, then, is the empty tomb? Pannenberg believes that the arguments we have just summarized stand as valid apart from the tradition of the empty tomb. Nevertheless, the latter is not to be dismissed as of no importance. Even granting that the tradition of the appearances and of the empty tomb were originally independent and only later combined, this does not necessarily mean that the empty tomb tradition is mere invention. Paul's silence about it is not conclusive. That the Jewish enemies of the faith could not produce the body is significant. One could hardly credit that the resurrection of Jesus could have taken place in Jerusalem except on the assumption that the tomb was empty. The subjective-vision hypothesis becomes even less probable, therefore. If the discovery of the empty tomb had been the cause of the disciples' flight to Galilee, which it was not, then we would have had to allow for the possibility of spontaneous visionary experiences induced in the disciples by their hope of the near end of the age and of the general resurrection of the dead which dominated their thinking before Jesus was put to death. If, however, the empty tomb was discovered after the Galilean appearances as an independent piece of evidence, this assumption would no longer be so convincing.[1] One is left with the impression that Pannenberg does not deny the empty tomb but holds that his description of the resurrection as historical would still stand on the basis of the appearances alone, even if the empty tomb were denied.

Pannenberg and Barth agree as against Bultmann that the resurrection of Jesus is a statement about reality. The rise of the faith in the risen Jesus is not simply identifiable with the reality of the resurrection. The latter, though known only to faith, is also the basis of faith since it points to a reality other than faith as the subjective appropriation of that reality. We believe both men to be right in this as against Bultmann. Barth, however, differs from Pannenberg in insisting that the affirmation of the resurrection of Jesus is not a historical judgement. To clarify this would require a whole treatise on the nature of history and of historical knowledge. Barth gets himself into obvious difficulties with his view of two kinds of history, one of which is subject to the canons of interpretation used by the historian, and one kind of history which is not so subject.

It is extremely difficult to leave the empty tomb on the fringe of our thought if it is asserted as both factual and significant. One could presumably say with some that it is not easy to explain it away as a late accretion of the tradition. One might also see it as a vivid and useful symbol of the fact that Jesus still really lives and not only in the subjective experiences of His disciples. Yet if the tomb was really empty, one can hardly avoid questions as to what happened to the body unless one is assuming that some other explanation is available of its emptiness, though we have no convincing historical evidence as to what that explanation might be. Dr Lampe believes that the evidence is convincing enough that there was an encounter between the disciples and Jesus alive after death which cannot be reduced only to a function of their psychology.[2] This, he believes, rests upon the undoubted experiential reality of the change in the disciples' faith and life between Good Friday and Easter. Dr Lampe also implies, though he does not explicitly say so, that this would have been just as true if the tomb was not empty and the body had seen corruption in the usual way.

Nevertheless, the fact remains that if it is insisted that the wonder of the resurrection-faith is that God has achieved for us the victory

[1] W. Pannenberg, *Jesus: God and Man*, pp. 100 ff.
[2] G. W. H. Lampe and D. M. Mackinnon, *The Resurrection*.

over death in the space-time world of actual history, then the problem is not so easily resolved. Dr Lampe is presumably convinced that the 'objective' reference of the resurrection appearances constitutes less of a problem for the modern man than the assertion of the empty tomb. But is this really so? If one is in earnest in affirming that the disciples were really in contact with a reality other than themselves (namely, Jesus as alive after death), then one is saying something which is as fantastic for modern psychology as the empty tomb may seem to be for physics and chemistry. A. E. Taylor long ago pointed out that such a stupendous breach of psychological law is as difficult to account for as a breach of physical law.[1] In both cases, a frank appeal is being made to the supernatural in the sense of an activity of God which does not fit into any normal causal explanation in the scientific sense. But, then, why not? We are back again with fundamental questions about God and His relation to the created order and whether the latter is an autonomous closed system of interacting forces which God may have set in motion but which He can no longer directly control or modify.

Some may object that our thesis is self-contradictory. On the one hand, we have attempted to show that Jesus and Paul both reject a literal, materialistic view of the resurrection of the righteous to a new life after death. On the other hand, we have not wanted to reject the empty tomb tradition and this means, therefore, if it means anything at all, that the resurrection of Jesus was in some sense physical. It seems, therefore, as if we are defending a non-physical type of resurrection for men in general and a physical or a quasi-physical one for Jesus. As we have already maintained, there is no *a priori* principle which demands that the resurrection of Jesus should be considered to be exactly the same as ours. For Jesus, the resurrection is not only a conviction that He is alive after death. It also includes the fact that He has manifested His reality and presence to men and women still living in this space-time world. After all, perhaps more was needed in the way of evidence for such an astonishing event if the disciples were to be assured of the fact and rescued from despair to a living hope.[2] There is, however, a basic ambiguity in the word 'physical'. As far as our own resurrection is concerned, we shall have occasion to argue later that the rejection of a literalistic physical resuscitation

[1] A. E. Taylor, *The Faith of a Moralist.*
[2] Especially if, as Evans contends in agreement with Bonsirven 'in the first Christian century, belief in resurrection was far from being commonly accepted among the Jews.' C. F. Evans, *Resurrection and the New Testament*, p .19.

does not necessarily mean the rejection of some concept of 'embodied' existence after death. In the case of Jesus, however, if the empty tomb is both a fact and integral to the resurrection, then in this single case His body did not see corruption, whereas our bodies do. M. E. Dahl has listed the objections which are usually made today against any suggestion that 'matter' can be rendered eternal, namely that it can have a destiny beyond this world, even in a transformed sense. If all 'matter' is ultimately dependent upon God for whatever form it takes now, and if we have abandoned 'billiard-ball' atoms for the modern concept of energy, there seems no reason in principle why the energies of matter in a particular physical form should not be capable of being directed to new and changed forms. We are not saying anything so naive as that modern physics proves the possibility of physical resurrection. We are saying, however, that given the Christian understanding of God and His relation to the total world-process, including what we call 'matter', there is no absurdity, scientific or otherwise, in the suggestion that the creative energy of God should not be capable of taking the whole man into a new form of existence beyond death which is an embodied existence, though very different from the one we now have. Nor again is there any *a priori* certainty that God could not enable a person in the resurrection mode of existence to manifest himself to men in this present cosmos. This could take place without that person's necessarily having to remain premanently on earth again in a body exactly similar to our present one. Dahl also contends that the Semitic totality concept precludes the idea that our bodies even now are material in the modern sense of the word.[1] This was an idea unknown to St Paul, Man is more than his body now, as we shall try to argue later on philosophical grounds. Dahl's further point, therefore, is well taken: 'Christian apologetics would do better, in this connection, to draw attention to the absurdity of suggesting that our personalities are simply "material" now, than to try to defend the proposition that they will be "material" then.'[2]

As far as this bears upon the resurrection of Jesus, it would seem that the Christian thinker should show a proper caution before dogmatically ruling out the possibility of Jesus having risen from the dead in the wholeness of His personal being with an appropriately embodied existence of which men on this side of death could be made aware. We are not under the illusion that we have 'proved' this to be the case with a simple knock-down argument based upon dubious

[1] M. E. Dahl, *The Resurrection of the Body*, Studies in Biblical Theology No. 36, p. 91.　　　　　　　　　　　　　　　　　　　　　　　[2] ibid., p. 91.

speculations derived from modern physics. All we are contending is that the case has not and cannot be closed on the basis of what modern science has said or some positivistic philosophies believe to be the case. Whether the possibility is a fact will depend upon several converging lines of evidence. The nature and reality of God, the force of the New Testament evidence, the moral and spiritual consequences of the Easter faith, the significance of the person of Jesus Christ. Obviously the force of the above evidence would not be compelling for any person, but we are not dealing with any person. We are dealing with Jesus Christ and the astonishing consequences of His impact upon the world and the life of men. His resurrection is, to say the least, appropriate to a life and death of such universal significance. Again we are not saying that because it is appropriate, therefore it was in fact so. We are suggesting, however, that our assessment of the evidence demands that we fully recognize that we are dealing with a unique phenomenon in history to which there is no real parallel, either before or since. What may seem ridiculously silly to claim for John Doe is not necessarily foolish for such a one as Jesus Christ.

It would seem, therefore, that in regard to the resurrection of Jesus, there are only certain options left open to us.

(1) We can say with Kaufmann that no man lives again after death in the fullness of personal existence and that this includes Jesus too. Jesus lives only in the influence He exerts upon the continuing history of man in this world.

(2) We can say with Lampe, and perhaps with Pannenberg, that the resurrection 'appearances' were a genuine encounter between the disciples and Jesus alive after death and that it would be reasonable to affirm this even if the tomb was not empty and the body of Jesus suffered corruption in exactly the same way as our bodies.

(3) We can try to defend the concept of resurrection as an 'embodied' existence and argue that in the case of Jesus, the energy of the physical body was transformed into a resurrection mode of existence and that Jesus was enabled by the power of God to make Himself known in the fullness of His manhood as the Victor over death and the divinely appointed Lord and Saviour of man.

We believe that the third option is to be preferred because it enables us to do more justice to the New Testament as a whole without an arbitrary mutilation of the documents or a dismissal of certain pieces of evidence because they do not fit certain scientific views which are themselves subject to constant change and modification.

Chapter Five

Man as more than His Body

In this chapter we shall break off our exposition of the Christian view on personal survival for a philosophical digression. This is necessary because any attempt to defend the Christian conviction on this point encounters deep-seated assumptions and indeed prejudices which many have never sat down and examined in a thoughtful way. It is not implied that we must turn to philosophy and science to find the backing for what is essentially uncertain and dubious in the Christian faith itself. The latter has its own peculiar evidence to which it summons men to give heed. For many contemporaries, however, it is difficult ever to get an open-minded appraisal of the Christian evidence because this initial step is rendered almost impossibly hard by their own unexamined assumptions. This chapter is to be seen, therefore, as a clearing of the ground in order to enable the reader to consider again the Christian claim without having dismissed the possibility of its truth beforehand for reasons which are not as conclusive as he thinks.

If we ask why belief in the survival of death is difficult for many modern men and women, there can be little doubt that it springs from our excessive concern with the body. Since science, by its very method, concentrates upon the investigation and exploration of nature in its physical aspects, it follows that when it comes to man, it tends to confine itself exclusively to his bodily existence and characteristics. No one questions this as a matter of method. The scientist is free to concentrate upon whatever aspect of the real world he considers to be most important at the time. Problems arise only when the conclusion is drawn that man is no more than his body. Many scientists cannot rightly be charged with such a sweeping statement as this, for they are often only too well aware of the mysteries which confront them, both in nature and in man, when scientific investigation has been carried to the limits of its present capacity. There can be no question, however, that the 'popular' view of science has tended to assume that 'science' can of necessity admit only body and never more than body.

There must, of course, be many other reasons which make it difficult for the average person in our age or in any age to believe in the possibility and reality of his survival of death. After all, most men and women are not philosophers, nor do they read books on the philosophy of science or theological tomes. Millions of people, however, do read popular magazines and journals, not to mention newspapers, in which articles on this question appear from time to time. They listen to lectures and panel discussions on TV and radio in which 'experts' express their views on all sorts of questions. There is, therefore, a wide and unprecedented dissemination of ideas, and the majority of people are exposed to them at some time or other. It is still, however, extremely difficult to know how many people do in fact have a positive conviction about their own survival of death. Questionnaires put out from time to time show a remarkable number still so believing, but obviously the results of such inquiries depend a great deal upon the age, educational level, intellectual sophistication and religious upbringing of the people who are interviewed. There are other factors too which influence all of us prior to more careful reflection, such as a natural tendency to define the real in terms of what which can be seen, touched, tasted, etc. This spontaneous 'materialism' or 'positivism' on the part of most people does not always preclude some vague belief in non-physical realities, even though no attempt is ever made by the person in question to think through what is involved or frame a satisfactory theory as to how these two aspects of reality can be related to each other. For most people, if the question of survival is ever consciously raised or considered, it usually takes the form of such questions as—will I survive death as recognizably 'me'? Will I be self-conscious, will I remember what happened to me in this life, will I recognize other people after death? What about babies who die young? Will they grow up in heaven? What about age? Will youth, middle age and old age mean anything in heaven? These may seem naive questions to a certain kind of sophisticated mind. Nevertheless, these are the questions which ordinary people ask if they can be persuaded to talk about the subject at all. And these questions are after all fundamental and basic, however simple their form. It is the question of the nature of personality, of self-identity, of the nature of self-consciousness, which is really being raised. Coupled with this issue are further questions which concern value rather than fact. Would it be worthwhile to survive death? The answer to this depends upon psychological factors in the person concerned. If a man finds life full, exciting and meaningful now, he may feel strongly that it would be splendid if it could be continued in some form. If, on the other hand, his experience is full of sorrow, frustration, despair, physical weakness and disability, or pain and disease, he might very well welcome death as a blessed release even if there is no after-life. Against this is to be set the reluctance to commit suicide on the part of millions whose lives in this world have been wretched in the extreme. Obviously, however, the issue as to whether a person really wants to survive death will be powerfully affected by the individual's belief as to the kind of life into which he thinks he will survive.[1]

It goes without saying that a consistent materialism will not have, indeed cannot have, any place for personal survival of death. It should, however, be made clear that this is only true of a materialism which regards all reality as material and all mental activity as reducible without remainder to physical process. As will be evident in our later discussion, the view that the self is dependent upon some kind of organ or body is quite compatible with some theories of resurrection. The only permanent and eternal reality for the consistent materialist will be matter itself, whether this latter is conceived of after the 'model' of billiard-ball atoms or in a more rarefied sense of some kind of 'energy'. How such matter came to be is a question not answered by such theories. It is just there, and persons are simply temporary ripples upon the surface of an ever-changing energy which is defined as non-mental, non-conscious and non-intelligent. Obviously, there can be no talk of personal survival on this basis. The only meaning that it could have would be that we survive as absorbed back into the eternal pool of energy from which for a brief time we emerged with an illusory sense of our self-identity. If the reader is interested in the critical evaluation of this kind of materialism, he is referred to some of the books listed below.[2]

It has to be admitted, however, that the word 'matter' is sometimes very loosely used. If such language is used as that matter has in it the potential to become mind, the result often is to attribute to matter so-called qualities and capacities which we only know as belonging to self-conscious mental activity. This, however, is cheating, since matter does not now mean that which is defined as non-mental, nor is it the matter with which physics is concerned. Matter then becomes

[1] A. Toynbee and others, *Man's Concern with Death*. Much interesting material is to be found in this volume concerning the universality of man's conviction as to some kind of survival of physical death.

[2] E. L. Mascall, *Christian Theology and Natural Science*. C. E. M. Joad, *Guide to Modern Thought*. E. Rogers, *Commentary on Communism*.

a mysterious source or process from which emerge ever-increasingly complex levels of existence, including mind. It may even be considered as having an intrinsic direction, nisus or *telos* which determines the direction, as in Marxism and some forms of progressive evolutionism.[1] It is doubtful whether this should be called a consistent materialism, for it allows for the emergence of new levels of activity, such as the mental, which are not reducible to the physical factors investigated by the physics of the day. It is often said that old-fashioned nineteenth-century materialism is not now defended by any outstanding philosopher or scientist. Few today would use such language as that used by Cabanis that 'the brain secretes thought as the liver secretes bile'.[2] Nevertheless, materialism often survives in a very sophisticated form which is not always recognized for what it is by the unwary reader. Professor H. D. Lewis has rendered a very valuable service in showing clearly the materialist implications of philosophical and psychological analyses which at first sight might appear to be otherwise.[3]

Let us return, then, to our principal theme—is man more than his body? Unless modern man can be convinced that this is a reasonable and possible statement to make about himself, he is hardly likely to have a mind open to those considerations which are decisive for Christian faith. If man is only body, then the latter's dissolution must mean the end of existence in any form. Christian theology has on the whole tended to think of man as a composite being, made up of body and soul. Yet as J. R. Lucas observes: 'There is a certain sense of uneasiness nowadays in talking about the soul'.[4] We have all heard the quip about modern psychology, that it first of all lost its soul, then its mind, and finally lost consciousness with J. B. Watson and the behaviourists. The only use which modern man seems to have for the word 'soul' is in such expressions as 'a soulful expression' or 'he has no soul', meaning he is devoid of feeling, insight, sympathy, etc. Surprisingly enough, it still turns up in some of the popular music of our day. For the more sophisticated it has lost its philosophical respectability, thanks to Gilbert Ryle's attack upon the 'ghost in the machine' and Descartes's suggestion that the point of contact between

---

[1] H. De Lubac, *The Religion of Teilhard de Chardin*. The above charge would not be legitimate against De Chardin who never excludes the teleological from the context of the divine activity. His *Phenomenon of Man* should be read in the light of his total work if it is to be properly assessed.

[2] W. McDougall, *Body and Mind* (Methuen, London, 1911), p. 83.

[3] H. D. Lewis, *The Elusive Mind*, cf. Chapter Four on 'The New Materialism'.

[4] B. Mitchell, *Faith and Logic*, p. 132.

the soul and the body is to be found in the pineal gland! There is nothing sacrosanct about a word. If soul is an embarrassment, let us drop it and concentrate on such questions as: Is man more than his body? Can mental activity be completely reduced to physical process? What is the nature of self-identity or my experience of being the same person enduring through the passage of time?

Before attempting to indicate how some modern thinkers have dealt with this problem, we shall digress for a moment into the area of biblical psychology. It has become a dogma of much so-called biblical theology in our time to stress the sharp distinction between the Hebrew doctrine of man and the dualist Greek view which divides man into body and soul. What has been called the 'Semitic totality concept' is taken to mean that man for Hebrew thought is conceived of as a unitary being to which such a dualism could not possibly apply. This, however, calls for the most careful analysis, nor must the 'emotive' use of the word dualist be allowed to settle the question out of hand. Because the Hebrew had the most vivid sense of the closest possible relationship between body and mind and found it difficult, at least in the early stages of Hebrew history, to conceive of a dis-embodied existence, does this mean that the Hebrew had no sense at all of the reality of the distinction between body and mind, or body and self, or body and soul? Did he deny an awareness of self-identity? When he engaged in thought, imagination, etc., did he imagine that he was only describing a bodily process and nothing more? Was he conscious of freedom and responsibility? Was he only a B C anticipation of a Marx or a Ryle or a modern behaviourist? Dr Wheeler Robinson, whose pioneer work in the field of Hebrew psychology is well known, pointed out a long time ago that the Hebrew did not sharply divide physiological from psychological in the manner we tend to do today. What we consider to be only a physical organ and no more, is linked by the Hebrew to psychical attributes. The breath-soul is the principle of life in man, but life here includes what we today would call mind and self-consciousness. Because heart, liver, kidney and bowels acquired a psychical use in Hebrew, this does not mean that the psychical was nothing more than the movements of these physical organs. Certainly an ethical dualism of good soul and evil body is remote from Hebrew thought. It is quite another thing to say that the distinction between physical and mental had no significance for the Hebrew in his own self-conscious experience. 'We may say, then, that the unity of personality, as conceived by the Hebrew, found its emotional expression chiefly under the name of nephesh, whilst intellectual and volitional activity centred on the heart (leb) as its organ'.[1]

The point to be noted here is that he did recognize the reality and distinctiveness of intellectual and volitional activity. Because of the limitations of his physiological knowledge and the lack of any clarification of the distinction between body and mind which more adequate knowledge and reflection would have compelled him to make, it does not mean that he did not know in experience the reality of the distinction. The awareness of self-identity and self-consciousness through memory and inner experience finds expression again and again in the accounts given by the Old Testament men of their experience as persons. Wheeler Robinson himself comments that while we must reject for primitive Hebrew psychology any explicit philosophical distinction of body and soul in the later sense. 'We do have a parallel theory of the conscious life of man, based on the primitive ideas of his body already indicated.'[2] The point again which we wish to emphasize is simply that the distinction of bodily and mental is there in Hebrew thought, albeit embodied in an inadequate, and from our point of view, a primitive, view of the body and its relationship to various psychical functions. The Hebrew was not a materialist or a behaviourist in his interpretation of the total activity of the human person.

It should also be observed that in speaking of what is possible or not possible for the Jewish mind, one should look at the whole history of Judaism, including the Christian era. To take the Hebrew view of the pre-exilic period as necessarily the only valid norm for what constitutes the 'Jewish mind' is obviously one-sided. That a particular view was held at a certain period, especially if it is earlier in time, does not of necessity demand the value-judgement that it is normative for all later developments. It is also strange how many biblical scholars who reject doctrines of literal interpretation and verbal inspiration nevertheless speak as if early Hebrew psychology is normative for us merely because it is in the Bible. Professor James Barr has some illuminating comments to make upon the often repeated assertion that it was impossible for Hebrew thought to arrive at or hold the idea of the separability and immortality of the soul as distinct from the body. 'But it is quite easy to show that in late Judaism the soul could be regarded as separate from the body.'[3] Wisdom 3: 1 and 4 Maccabees show this tendency, to mention only the most familiar. Nor, as Barr

[1] H. W. Robinson, *The Christian Doctrine of Man*, p. 26.   [2] ibid., p. 20.
[3] J. Barr, *Old and New in Interpretation*, p. 52.

observes, is it self-evident that this was always due to Hellenistic influence. It may very well have been the result of tensions and problems within Judaism itself.[1] Nor again is this tendency confined only to extra-canonical Judaism. The fact, as we have seen, that Jesus could think of the resurrection life as not involving the giving and receiving in marriage certainly suggests a mode of existence remarkably different from our present physical one. Barr contends both resurrection and immortality could be affirmed together (cf. Matt. 10: 28; Luke 12: 4 ff.; Luke 22: 43 ff.). This means at the least that no absolute dichotomy between the two conceptions can be affirmed. Even in rabbinic sources, ideas of the pre-existence of the incorporeal soul can be found. Further, Greek thought is not of one mind on the subject. Plato can be cited in favour of the separability of the soul from the body and its continued existence after death. Aristotle, on the other hand, with his view of the soul as the form of the body, is much nearer to some modern conceptions of the more sophisticated behaviourist kind. Barr also criticizes Cullmann[2] for the suggestion that the opposition to Paul's teaching at Athens was due to the critics' adherence to the doctrine of the immortality of the soul. This would be so only if they were Platonists, and there is no evidence that they were. They are described as 'Stoics and Epicureans' (Acts 17: 32). The former probably thought of the individual as absorbed again at death into the cosmic process. The latter's atomic theory was a form of materialism which involved the complete dissolution of the indivual at death.[3] They were not, therefore, rejecting Paul's doctrine of resurrection in favour of the immortality of the soul. They were rejecting the idea of the survival of death by the individual in any form.

We have summarized Professor Barr's comments at some length because they are of far-reaching importance for our subject. What distinguished late Judaism from Greek thought was not its firm adherence to resurrection as opposed to immortality. 'The anthropological conceptions did not have kerygmatic status.'[4] This means that a Jew of this period was not accused of heresy or 'deviationism' or disloyalty to the faith if he opted for some version of the immortality of the soul. One could argue that Judaism should have made it a confessional test and that a doctrine of resurrection should have been an article of faith by which the Jewish 'church' stood or fell in its relationships with the Gentile world of thought. As a matter of

---

[1] J. Barr, op. cit., p. 52.
[2] O. Cullmann, *Immortality of the Soul or Resurrection of the Dead?*
[3] Barr, op. cit., p. 54. [4] ibid., p. 53.

historical fact, however, this was not the case. This means that the question of resurrection and/or immortality can be judged on its merits without its being prematurely settled by the assertion that one is Hebrew and the other Greek, and that the former view is naturally binding upon us. The basic question, therefore, will need to be differently formulated. What view of the after-life is most consonant with the biblical view of God, the teaching of Jesus and our present knowledge of the nature of man and the mind-body relationship? Since, therefore, neither Judaism at all stages of its historical development nor Jesus Himself can be cited in favour of resurrection as involving the continuance of the physical body in its present form after death, we are free to take a fresh look at the whole question.

After this somewhat lengthy digression, we shall now return to our discussion of the problem of the 'self' in relation to the body. After all, it is ambiguity and uncertainty on this point which is the most powerful factor in influencing modern man to take a negative view of the possibility of survival of death, whether such survival takes the form of resurrection or immortality or some attempted fusion of the two ideas. Two basic questions call for discussion:

(a) Can a case still be made for a 'substantival' view of the self?

(b) Is the relationship of the self to the body such that it is impossible to conceive of its continued existence when separated from its physical body?

It is often assumed that a negative answer to both these questions is demanded by our modern biological and psychological understanding of man. In our view, this is by no means the case. If this can be substantiated, it does not, of course, justify us in deducing immediately the reality of the personal survival of death, apart from all considerations relative to the truth and validity of the Christian claim about our knowledge of God. It does mean, however, that the possibility of such survival cannot be ruled out beforehand out of deference to an authoritative scientific view assumed to be the common mind of all contemporary scientists and philosophers.

In attempting to answer the above two questions, the gap between the technical language of the philosopher and ordinary language today becomes a fruitful source of misunderstanding. It is necessary to be quite clear about the meaning of the questions themselves. What is intended by the question whether we can still defend the 'substantival' view of the self? Let it be clearly stated that it has nothing to do with physical substance, which is the way the ordinary person today would understand it. When classical Christian theology spoke of God as 'one substance', as it did in the Latin form of the doctrine of the Trinity, or when some philosophers speak of the soul or self as a substance, they did not and do not mean a physical entity. Indeed, one might say in general that the very reverse of this was intended. To argue for a 'substantialist' view of the self is to maintain that the self is an enduring entity of some kind which is more than the sum of the experiences which occur in it and to it. Furthermore, the 'I' of personal identity cannot be reduced to or explained solely by changes in the physical body, however closely it is linked to that body in our present existence.

It might very well be asked why anyone should wish to question such an obvious fact of experience. The fact remains that many have questioned it and still do. In answering such critics, Professor C. A. Campbell has insisted that 'self-consciousness is a fact, a datum from which we have to start'.[1] He claims that every knowing or cognizing subject is in some degree self-conscious, that there is an awareness of being the self-same being throughout our different experiences.[2] On the basis of this given awareness, we speak quite naturally of the 'I' which has these experiences. Yet as everyone knows, this spontaneous ascription of our experiences to an enduring 'I' which is somehow more than just a series of experiences has been questioned many times: by Buddhists in ancient times, by Hume in the eighteenth century and by many today who are influenced by Hume and by what they believe to be demanded by the scientific study of man and his body in particular. It is important to realize that the scientific study of man demands that the scientist take the standpoint of an outside or external observer. When the scientist looks at another human being, he does not see with his naked eye that person's consciousness or his self-awareness. He only studies his physical and bodily behaviour. It is not difficult to understand how such an exclusive preoccupation with the 'outside' of the person should lead to doubts about the reality of the 'I' or the 'self' of that other person as known in his self-consciousness. The psychologist, if he refuses the testimony of introspection, is likewise committed to this 'external' view of the individual. Of course, it is always possible to remind the scientific observer that he too is man, and that if he frankly examines his self-consciousness, he will have no doubt about his own 'I'. It is astonishing, however, how often a certain type of mind forgets this altogether, as if science were carried on by some impersonal process of

[1] C. A. Campbell, *On Selfhood and Godhood*, p. 81.   [2] ibid., p. 77.

investigation and not by self-conscious persons, namely scientific 'men'.[1]

If, then, we are going to speak meaningfully about the 'self', we must abandon this stance of an apparent impersonal observer and concentrate upon our own experience of self-awareness. This means having recourse to introspection, looking within, and not merely to observation of physical behaviour patterns. Such introspection is obviously a highly personal and individual affair. No one can do it for us. It has to be our own act. No one else can look directly into our consciousness. Because of the difficulty of subjecting the act and the content of introspection to the precise types of measurement which are possible when dealing with physical things, including the body, it has often been highly unpopular in some scientific circles. The more extreme type of behaviourist has ruled it out as incapable of giving us any kind of reliable knowledge of a 'self' known to us in self-consciousness. This is an extreme position to which many would not want to adhere today, though those who repudiate such a position in theory as a matter of method often seem to end with a denial of the 'self'. That the issue is still a very live one is shown by the appearance of such a book as listed below.[2]

It is well known, however, that even if we admit the validity of introspection for discovering the reality and nature of the self, the latter is often explained away as no more than a fiction, useful to describe the continuous series of psychological states which go to make up our human experience. Some years ago, the late C. E. M. Joad used two illustrations to help the layman appreciate the import of Hume's criticism of the self. When we look at the cinema screen, we see apparently continuous figures which remain the same throughout the film. We know, however, that we are looking at a series of separate static figures on a roll of film which give the illusion of sameness and identity through change when run off in quick succession. So with us. 'We' are only successions of experiences which are contiguous in time and resemble each other. We find it convenient to believe that there is an 'I', an enduring 'self' which remains throughout the experiences. This, however, though understandable from a psychological point of view, is not so in fact. There is no real 'I' above and beyond the chronological sequence of experiences. Or, as he puts it in another way, if we think of the self as a necklace,' the effect of Hume's criticism is to eliminate the thread and leave only the beads.'[3] It is

---

[1] M. Polanyi, *Personal Knowledge.*
[2] C. V. Borst (ed.), *The Mind/Brain Identity Theory.*
[3] C. E. M. Joad, *Guide to Philosophy*, p. 233.

argued that if this seems odd and unconvincing to most of us, that does not necessarily prove it wrong. On the other hand, if it makes nonsense of the universal and persistent awareness of selfhood which all men have, and if in practice, as even Hume admitted, we act as if the 'I' were not an illusion, then it seems rather foolish to allow such a theory to explain away what seems to be the undoubted realities of self-awareness and self-identity. The fact that we cannot 'introspect our own act of introspection', that we cannot look within and see the 'I' as a distinguishable object, does not disprove its reality. The 'I' is not a physical object. One cannot take a photograph of it or measure it with physical instruments. We do not have to strain to see with the physical eye a mysterious something over and above our experiences. 'The consciousness of oneself as a unique and irreducible being or of self-identity in its most basic sense, is thus given with, is irretrievably involved in, the distinctiveness of having experience of any kind.'[1]

How important is this issue? Does it have any important practical implications for the living of our daily lives or is it a matter which we can leave the philosophers to discuss happily among themslves? It is in fact of the utmost practical importance, especially where it bears upon the exercise of our freedom and our sense of moral responsibility. Without getting ourselves involved again at this point in a discussion of the age-old problem of freewill versus determinism,[2] it does seem evident that if there is no 'I' in the above sense, then it is difficult to see how we could speak of freedom and responsibility. If there is no sense in which I can consider myself to be the same person I was ten years ago, then equally it is ridiculous to feel any sense of responsibility for acts done that long ago. How can a stream of psychical events be conscious of itself as such a sequence? And if the only continuity is a bodily one, what my body did ten years ago is of no concern to me. Indeed, what could 'me' mean in this case?

Now this does seem to run contrary to the spontaneous conviction of most people. Shame, guilt, moral approval or disapproval are experienced by us now in regard to acts done many years ago. We do not seem to be able to shake off our links with that person who in more than a formal sense is continuous with my present 'I'. Some no doubt would say—so much the worse for our so-called sense of freedom and responsibility. But this is surely an arbitrary and cavalier way of dismissing one of the most persistent aspects of human

---

[1] H. D. Lewis, *The Elusive Mind*, p. 234 (see the rest of this book for a brilliant defence of the above quoted statement).

[2] Cf. A. Farrer, *The Freedom of the Will*.

experience. To deny any non-material element in our make-up, whether we call it mind, soul, spirit, or self, is really to render our experience incoherent. If all our behaviour is explainable solely in terms of changes in the physical body or a sequence of psychological states rooted ultimately in these physical changes, then the very notion of truth, whether philosophical, scientific, psychological, moral or any other becomes impossible. 'Rival theories of psychology merely reflect the conditions prevalent in the bodies of rival psychologists. To ask which of the theories is true is as meaningless as to ask which of the various blood pressures of the theorists concerned is true.'[1] All theories are but reflections of bodily states and we can do nothing about that! Despite the force of these objections, the old materialism dies hard. Despite the more sophisticated views of modern scientists and many philosophers, it is still assumed by many today that 'science' teaches that man is no more than his body. The self's survival of death is hardly likely to get fair discussion because of this dogma that we cannot know whether there is a 'self' now, not to mention whether it can continue in being after death. This brings us to the second question that was asked: Is the relationship of the self to the body such that it is impossible to conceive of its continued existence when separated from its physical base in the body which we now have? At this point we have to be very clear as to the distinction between what it is legitimate to say on the basis of a reasonable analysis of our experience, conducted by the scientist, philosopher, etc., and what it would be legitimate to say if the Christian faith were true.

As far as the former is concerned, a very strong case can be made for the view that man is more than his body. There is no established empirical evidence from the sciences which compels us to deny the equally empirical facts of self-consciousness, awareness of self-identity, memory, freedom and the facts of moral obligation. In our practical experience, no one questions the intimate link between the self so conceived and the body. There would seem, however, to be no compelling reason why the self should not continue without this body in its present form. We are not at the moment saying that it does in fact so continue to exist. We are simply maintaining that the idea is not intrinsically absurd and that the facts of our present experience do not rule it out as unworthy of consideration. Such a continued existence of the self without the present body might be inconceivable in the sense that we cannot frame a detailed imaginative

[1] C. E. M. Joad, *Guide to Modern Thought*, p. 61.

picture of what such a disembodied existence might be. It is not inconceivable if the implication is that we cannot make sense of the idea of its possibility at least.

It is important to realize what follows from our previous argument. Even if, for various reasons, we come to the conclusion that it is highly unlikely that the 'self' would continue to exist without a body of some kind, this would still not make the self to be only 'body'. As long as the term body is being used, in however analogical a way, to indicate the sort of processes which are akin to those we know here, we would still have to say that in the next life the self is more than its body, even if we use such terms as resurrection body or astral body, following some theosophists and spiritualists. This is about as far as we can go with this kind of discussion. If there is anything more that can be said, it will depend upon whether we think something has been made known to us about God and His purpose which gives grounds for further statements about the survival of the individual after death. This means that the appeal cannot be made on empirical grounds in the very narrow sense of the word given to empirical in the 'empiricist' tradition. The question of resurrection/immortality is primarily a religious and not a scientific question. This does not mean that the investigation of such phenomena as telepathy, E.S.P. or the data afforded by spiritualist mediums can be simply dismissed or that they might not throw interesting new light upon existence after death. Such evidence must be judged on its merits. Nor does it mean that all scientific thought leads of necessity to a 'materialistic' philosophy, for we have seen that this is not the case. The question of immortality or resurrection is religious in the sense that the existence of the self after death raises questions, not only about the continuance of that self in being, but about the quality of that existence in moral and spiritual terms. After all, one could conceive of an existence after death which might be as absurd and as frustrating as some people seem to find the present life. The religious man, and the Christian in particular, is not concerned merely with going on and on in some form of existence other than the present one. He is concerned with that spiritual transformation of the self into conformity with the image of Christ which alone gives full meaning to human existence, whether here or beyond death. Quality is of decisive importance in the Christian view of things.

It does not follow, however, as some modern Christians seem to think, that it does not matter whether we survive death or not. They say we can have the Christian quality of life even now, and even if this is the only life we have. This is true but only partially so. In this life, even if we are in Christ, we are still pressing toward the mark. We are not yet perfect and we have not yet attained. To make death the end is to leave us spiritually immature and incomplete, even if we are believers, and condemns many whose present lives have been mainly frustration and disappointment to an annihilation which denies them self-fulfilment or realization of their God-given potentialities. Yet now we are speaking in the full context of the Christian faith accepted and believed. The questions we have raised earlier about the 'self' are still of momentous importance. H. H. Price has rightly stressed that to ignore consciousness and all that goes with it is to end with the depersonalizing of man. His remarks are so wise and relevant to our previous discussion that I quote at some length:

The respect which we have for persons surely has something to do with the belief that each person has a private inner life of his own, and cannot easily be retained if that belief is abandoned . . . for religion will never flourish in a philosophical atmosphere where the inner life which is distinctive of persons is neglected.[1]

[1] I. T. Ramsey, *Biology and Personality*, p. 209.

Chapter Six

Resurrection or Immortality

Our previous discussion of the nature of personal survival of death has led to conclusions which in our judgement must be decisive for any further speculation we wish to undertake. We are not in fact claiming that all the scientific and philosophical questions connected with the 'self' and 'self-identity' have been finally and exhaustively answered. Our claim is simply that the present philosophical climate of opinion is now open enough to permit the Christian to offer his own answers as illuminations of the problems which are deserving of serious consideration. In the case of the Bible and of the New Testament in particular, we have seen that the latter, though still using the language of resurrection, reinterprets it in a sense which points away from a doctrine of resuscitation of the identical physical body. Neither Jesus nor Paul would appear to be committed to a view of the resurrection body as simply the unchanged continuance after death of that same body which we now possess. Philosophy, while it cannot demonstrate that the soul or self is intrinsically immortal in the Platonic sense, can at the least show the enormous difficulties inherent in a materialistic and naturalist view of man. Mental process is not simply reducible to physical process. Furthermore, no adequate and intelligible psychology can be constructed on the basis of the elimination of the self and its continuing identity.[1] Science, as distinct from a philosophy of science which attempts a total view of the world and therefore becomes a philosophy, is not in a position to be dogmatic about the issue of survival. It can point out that even if soul, self or mind is irreducible to physical process, yet we have no reliable experience of disembodied selves or minds, as far as this life is concerned, even if the person is more than his body. It is true that claims have been made both in ancient and modern times for the having of 'out of the body' experiences. The reader is referred to interesting material in Arnold Toynbee's *Man's Concern with Death*. We are not settling this question with a merely dogmatic denial, but pointing out that in the

[1] J. Ward, *Psychological Principles*. F. R. Tennant, *Philosophical Theology*, vol. I.

absence of an agreed interpretation of these phenomena by scientists, philosophers and theologians, the Christian would be well advised not to attempt to base his convictions about life after death upon the claims made for this type of experience. It is clear that all this does not add up to a categorical denial either of the possibility or the reality of survival of death. The question is left open and we are still free to ask if there are any religious considerations which enable us to go beyond the proper agnosticism of the philosopher and the scientist. The question of survival should not be solved until all the evidence is in. The thesis we are about to argue is that for the Christian, anything he says about the life after death will be deduction from what he now knows about God. It is not directly concerned with empirical evidence in the restricted sense in which the word 'empirical' is now used. If this were the case, we would have to concentrate upon spiritualistic phenomena, E.S.P. and other hitherto unexplained psychic phenomena. On this point, at least, we agree with Schleiermacher that in this case, the doctrine of immortality would belong to the higher natural science, and the certainty of it would depend upon those who had mastered scientific method.[1] We should accept it from them upon authority, just as the modern layman accepts Einstein's theory on the authority of the scientific community, not because he understands it.

On the other hand, the word 'empirical' has become so closely linked with a certain kind of philosophy that it is often assumed that if we do not claim empirical evidence for our belief in God, for example, we are implying that there is no evidence which could commend the belief other than by an appeal to wishful thinking. If we could persuade all philosophers to use the word empirical in the broader sense recommended by Professor John Smith,[2] then it would be quite in order to claim that the eschatological deductions made from our belief in God are rooted empirically in the present knowledge of God.

We shall be seeking in this chapter to draw out the implications of the Christian view of resurrection and to grapple with the question as to what kind of language is most appropriate to express this view. It is as well to remind ourselves again of the distinction between meaning and the language we use to convey that meaning. What do we want to say on the basis of Christian faith, and then, how shall we say it? We cannot remain entirely silent and inarticulate, otherwise the meaning vanishes from our grasp. We are face to face with the

[1] F. Schleiermacher, *The Christian Faith*, tr. H. R. Mackintosh and J. S. Stewart, p. 698. [2] J. E. Smith, *Reason and God*, p. 144.

problem which confronts any kind of religious discourse. We must 'symbolize' our meaning, linguistically or otherwise. On the other hand, we have to recognize that our symbols, analogies, and myths borrow their material from our experiences in this space-time world. Their application to existence beyond death will of necessity require some qualifications. We have seen that Jesus already recognized this fact in His reinterpretation of the resurrection of the body in a manner which distinguished it from a literal, physical resuscitation of the present body. When Christians adopt this line of interpretation, there-fore, they are not necessarily employing an idea derived from alien philosophical sources. They are following the Master Himself. Further, Jesus' reinterpretation did not involve any denial of continu-ing self-identity in the next life. God is the God of Abraham, Isaac and Jacob, of Tom, Dick and Harry.

Professor H. D. Lewis has commented on the obscurity and ambiguity which often surrounds the discussion of this question of survival in recent literature. One is often not clear whether a quality of this present life only is meant, or whether a reference is being made to the existence of persons after death. Even if we insist that conditions in the next life will be very different from those in this life, we are at the very least asserting some kind of existence of persons after death. 'If we have life eternal, we must *be* in some way after death.'[1] It is concerning this 'existence' after death with which we are primarily concerned here. This is not to deny that we might speak in a meaningful way about eternal life as a quality of life in the present. The New Testament does talk in this way and we have no wish to deny it or to underestimate its importance. There is, however, a proper distinction to be made between qualitative eternal life now and the future existence of persons after death. Whatever we may say about the limitations and inadequacy of temporal language, we are implying that persons now dead are still alive somehow and have existence of some kind. It is with this issue that we are now concerned. Of course, the Christian is concerned with the 'quality' of existence in the next life, for this is implied in the very notion of being 'in Christ'.

It is well to admit frankly that if the Christian believes that he will 'be' in some real sense after death, he does so on the basis of his faith in the power of God to secure his continuance in existence. He does not ground his belief on a philosophical demonstration or upon em-pirical evidence supplied by psychical research. He puts his confidence

[1] H. D. Lewis, *Philosophy of Religion*, p. 316.

in the God who raised Jesus Christ from the dead. It is obvious that anyone who is basically sceptical about that claim will not be able or willing to affirm what the Christian affirms about an after-life. We are not implying that faith lacks all cognitive claims or that rational considerations cannot be advanced on behalf of the Christian faith.[1] What is simply being stated is that one can hardly expect men to affirm Christian conclusions from non-Christian premises. Whether the Christian premises can be defended on broad rational grounds is a question which must be discussed on its merits. Langdon Gilkey is certainly right to insist that the crucial element in the present 'secular' atmosphere is 'this weakening of the cognitive certainty of personal faith'.[2] Whether this secular mood is the norm for the assessment of all Christian belief is itself another question. The Christian indeed must deny that it is, which does not mean that he is falling back upon sheer irrationality.

A good case might be made, along the lines indicated already, that philosophy and science do not supply conclusive negative evidence against the Christian claim. One might argue that they do point positively in that direction, but the full Christian claim can only rest on what the Christian affirms about the 'way things are' on the basis of that kind of evidence which deserves to be taken seriously into account. We have no wish to try to convince the agnostic or the atheist that he is really a Christian at heart or, as John Baillie asserted, a believer at the bottom of his heart, even when he denies it with the 'top of his mind'. This would imply that it is a matter of indifference how a man assesses the Christian evidence, or that the evidence is of no real importance when a decisive judgement has to be made. However, before we can ask the doubter to consider the Christian case, an attempt must be made to state clearly what the case is, so that the knows what he is being asked to accept or reject.

This requires, among other things, some clarification of Christian language. Shall we continue to use either the language of resurrection or that of immortality, or can we combine both without contradiction? It must be admitted that this clarification has very often not been made, with the result that both believer and unbeliever are not always clear as to what is involved or what is at stake. As our previous study has already shown, there are some modern Christian thinkers, though still a minority, who start from the dogmatic premise that 'dead men do not live again'. We have given our reaction to this position and

[1] cf. H. P. Owen, *The Christian Knowledge of God.*
[2] L. Gilkey, *Naming the Whirlwind; the Renewal of God-Language*, p. 117.

found it wanting on both scriptural and other grounds. This strong denial of any existence of any kind after death needs to be distinguished from the position of those who concentrate upon eternal life as a quality of present existence. Those who belong to this latter group do not necessarily dogmatically deny that this quality of existence might possibly continue in an order or realm of being very different from the space-time context in which we now find ourselves. Sometimes, however, the issue is left vague and ambiguous, and the dividing-line between those who stress eternal life now and those who categorically deny the possibility of any kind of personal existence after death sometimes wears rather thin. It is obviously unfair to generalize and we shall try to clarify the issues by discussing selected Christian thinkers who have dealt with our theme.

Among those who deny that dead men live again after death, Professor Gordon Kaufman is the most notable contemporary representative among Christian thinkers. We have considered his position in detail earlier in our investigation and we shall not repeat our criticisms here. The chief difference between Kaufman and a simple denial of the after-life, as in Corliss Lamont's humanist treatment of the subject,[1] is that the former interprets history in the light of the holy, righteous and loving purpose of a transcendent God but confines the realization of that purpose to historical existence. Lamont would presumably interpret history from the perspective of certain human values which elicit his loyalty and constitute his 'faith'. If our analysis is correct of the Hebrew psychology and of the later Greek influence upon Jewish thought, not to mention the views of Jesus Himself, then it is possible to speak of resurrection without meaning literal resuscitation of the present body. It is also possible to adapt the language of immortality to indicate the survival of the person. Part of the confusion arises from the fact that it is often assumed that the Greek idea of immortality implies an existence after death which is that of the bare intellect or mind. This is then contrasted unfavourably with resurrection on the grounds that the immortality offered is too intellectual, too bloodless and thin to be of any real interest. Who really wants to survive only as bare intellect or a concept in the divine mind?

This point is made very strongly by Norman Pittenger: 'The resurrection of the dead, then, is the Christian hope—not simply the immortality of the soul.'[2] He then goes on immediately to tell us that

---

[1] Corliss Lamont, *The Illusion of Immortality*.
[2] W. N. Pittenger, *God in Process*.

this, of course, does not mean that we survive death with material bodies, that the physics, chemistry and biology of our present physical bodies are not involved. What, then, is the advantage in retaining the language of resurrection except for the purely psychological reason that this is the kind of language to which Christians have been accustomed for many centuries? Pittenger's answer seems to be that the language of resurrection preserves more adequately than the language of immortality the idea that we survive death with the 'full integrity of our humanity', that our total experience in the body here and now must somehow be preserved in the life beyond.[1] Furthermore, the importance of social relationships in the after-life is better preserved by the language of resurrection, because in this life such relationships are mediated through the body. All this may be true but, if so, it needs to be recognized that such a view is not as far removed from some views of immortality as he thinks. Neither immortality nor resurrection in his view involves the retention of the present body.

While it is possibly true that some philosophical ideas of immortality suffer from this kind of anaemia, there would seem to be no intrinsic reason why this should be so. It is doubtful, for example, whether the charge would be fair to Plato. Even if it were so, it could still be legitimate for the Christian to talk of immortality and mean by it a fullness of personal existence that has not been intellectualized away to a mere shadow of itself. It is highly doubtful whether Aristotle was committed to personal survival of death if this means that some kind of individual self-consciousness continues. He was not a dualist in the Platonist sense and is much nearer to modern empiricism in seeing the soul as the 'form' of the body, as the integrating, organizing principle of the body. Nowhere does he suggest the possibility of the soul existing as separate from the body. If any kind of immortality is envisaged other than the fact of the eternity of the Prime Mover, it probably meant for Aristotle the re-absorption of the divine part of man (that is the reason) into its original divine and transcendent source. In any case, his position is far removed from that of Plato or of later Christian belief.[2] The problem of religious language returns to challenge us. Can the language of resurrection still be used without implying the continuance of the present physical body unchanged in the after-life? Can the language of immortality still be used without suggesting a weakening of the notion of full personal existence, including the significance of social relationships?

[1] W. N. Pittenger, *God in Process*, p. 88.
[2] J. Choron, *Death and Western Thought*, pp. 52 ff.

It is interesting to observe how different Christian thinkers have reacted in varied ways to these issues. It is noteworthy that the late Dr H. Wheeler Robinson, an acknowledged Hebrew scholar of this century, opted for immortality despite his long-standing preoccupation with the Hebrew scriptures. 'The term "immortality" is preferable to "resurrection" because our whole line of thought points to the immortality of the soul and its values rather than to the resurrection of the body.'[1] On this point, he tells us, 'Greek thought contributes more than the Hebrew unless we follow up Paul's idea of a spiritual body which he interprets as not involving the continuance of the present physical body'.[2] However, despite his strong insistence on spiritual values, Dr Robinson is not content to leave these values floating in the void or to anchor them only in God in an abstract way. He contends that Christian faith and experience must insist on the individuality of the concept of personality and that under no circumstances can this be surrendered. This means that the individuality of personality will be preserved in the after-life. Nor does Dr Robinson mean by individuality an atomistic society of unrelated units. He realizes full well that person and community are correlative and that each is meaningless when detached from the other. We believe this to be in accord with the teaching of Jesus and of the New Testament generally, not to mention the main stream of Christian thinking from then until now. If this is what is meant by the personal survival of death, it seems a matter of relative indifference whether we call it resurrection or immortality. In any case, the persistence of the physical body in its present form is not intended, nor does immortality mean a dissolving away of the individuality of personal existence. The question then becomes the purely practical one as to which kind of language leads to the least misunderstanding. Our own preference is for immortality in an 'embodied form' where the use of the latter phrase demands that we explain what we mean. The language of resurrection still suggests to many people that the body will be retained with all its present organs after death. The theologians might continue to use the language of resurrection, in which case they must explain carefully to the non-theologians what they mean. There is no reason why the language of resurrection should not be used, provided it is recognized that neither Jesus nor Paul intend to suggest a literal resuscitation of the present body.

We shall now turn our attention to the more recent reflections of Paul Tillich on this same subject. He is chosen here because of his

[1] H. W. Robinson, *The Christian Doctrine of Man*, p. 286.   [2] ibid., p. 287.

theological stature, the extensiveness of his influence, and his acknowledged indebtedness to the Greek tradition. He is also a good object of study concerning this issue of personal survival because of the striking ambiguities of his thought. In this he is typical of much modern Christian thinking, but it is of special value to see the reasons for this as exhibited in the work of a thinker of such admitted depth and penetration. We shall concentrate chiefly upon the relevant sections of his *Systematic Theology*.[1] On the matter of language, he reminds us of the fact already observed that only 'resurrection' is biblical language, while admitting the powerful influence of the Greek idea of immortality upon later Christian thinking. While he believes that the phrase 'resurrection of the body' can still be used, it is clear that it is given a very sophisticated reinterpretation which would be very puzzling to the simple believer if he really understood what Tillich was saying. It is also clear that he is opposed to any understanding of eternal life as a 'life hereafter', whether this be expressed in the language of resurrection or immortality. He does not appear to be saying simply that temporal language cannot be used in a naive way of life after death, as if the latter were merely a continuation of our present existence. He seems to be denying in a categorical way any idea of the preservation of the individuality of personal existence after death, such as we found defended by Wheeler Robinson. Immortality, says Tillich, is not a natural quality of the human soul. On this point, he is against Plato and all Christian thinkers who have followed his lead. If eternal life, and for Tillich this has a predominantly qualitative meaning, is real at all, it is rather a 'creative act of God who lets the temporal separate itself from and return to the eternal.'[2] The crucial question is: what exactly does this kind of language mean for Tillich?

It would take us too far afield to discuss in detail whether Tillich's Ground of Being is exactly what the Bible or most Christians have understood by God. His 'God beyond God'[3] and his obvious fear of a too naive application of personal analogies to God may well make us hesitate. It seems reasonably clear that the 'Ground of Being' for him cannot be described by such phrases as timeless or endless time. 'God' is not finite, neither is 'He' subject to temporal process. God in a literal sense is beyond all symbols which are taken from temporal existence or the human experience of 'time'. Yet all comes from the

---

[1] P. Tillich, *Systematic Theology*, vol. iii, pp. 409 ff.

[2] ibid., p. 410.

[3] P. Tillich, *The Courage to Be*.

Eternal and returns to the Eternal: eternal here, it must be remembered, signifying that which radically transcends temporality in any form conceivable by man. If this is so, then one would have expected that the only way in which temporality can be taken into God is by its radical destruction as temporality. Yet since the individuality of personal finite creatures seems bound up with at least some 'form' of space and time, if only to make room for real distinctions between one creature and another, then it would seem to follow that individuality can have no real place in the 'ground of Being' as eternal. Perhaps this is what Tillich really intends to say, and if so, it would justify Professor H. D. Lewis's remark that 'the proper place for Tillich and many of his followers today is in the Hindu religion.'[1]

If this seems a harsh judgement upon one who claims to be a Christian thinker, let us see if Tillich had other things to say which might modify our first impression. It is extremely difficult to give a résumé or exposition of Tillich's position, since in that part of Volume Three where he treats of this subject there is a truly bewildering interweaving of ideas. The smoothness of the style at first gives the impression that a genuine synthesis of these ideas has been achieved. A closer look, however, begins to raise doubts. It is possible to select passages which the unwary reader might take to be a simple restatement of the survival of death by the individual as a self-conscious person. He tells us that everything temporal has a 'teleological relation to the eternal, but man is the only creature who is consciously aware of this fact'.[2] He assures us that after the prophetic demythologization of the sphere of the gods into the One who is the ground and aim of everything that is, our finitude does not cease to be finitude, but it is 'taken into' the infinite, the eternal.[3] Does this mean that self-conscious persons survive death? It is by no means clear. Tillich agrees that Christian theology could not follow the Plotinian mystical line of absorption into the One because of 'its [i.e. Christianity's] emphasis upon the individual person and his eternal destiny'.[4] Yet immediately afterwards he attacks Christian theology for risking the superstitious consequences of employing the Greek idea of the immortality of the soul. Locke, Hume and Kant are cited as justified in their criticism, which was not an attack upon the symbol 'immortality' but on the concept of a naturally immortal substance, the soul. This seems a very charitable judgement, at least of Hume. The latter's

[1] H. D. Lewis and R. L. Slater, *World Religions*, p. 195.
[2] P. Tillich, *Systematic Theology*, vol. iii, p. 406.
[3] ibid., p. 411. [4] ibid., p. 411.

destructive attack upon the self and its real identity through experience would seem to be as fatal to any doctrine of man in his present life as it would be equally exclusive of any survival of the 'self' in another life. Be this as it may, Tillich is convinced that eternal life must be liberated from its dangerous connection with the concept of the immortal soul.[1] The idea of resurrection can hardly fare any better in his thought if it, too, suggests the survival of the person as a self-conscious individual. Still less does it mean for Tillich the continuance of the present physical body. Are we justified in interpreting Tillich's aversion to the concept of the immortal soul or a physical resurrection as equivalent to the denial of self-conscious individuals after death? My own feeling is that we are so justified, though one can never be absolutely sure with Tillich. 'The Eternal', he tells us, 'is not a future state of things.'[2] On the other hand: 'Eternal life is still life and the universal centredness does not dissolve the individual centres.'[3]

At first sight, this looks like a clear affirmation of the reality of self-conscious persons after death. When, however, a closer look is taken, doubts again begin to rise. Tillich attacks very vigorously the idea of a twofold eternal destiny which involves blessedness or loss of it as a reality which individual persons can know and experience. It is not only that he dislikes the Calvinist double decree and the obvious moral difficulties attending that particular view of election and predestination. The very idea of any absolute (does this mean final?) judgement upon human persons is objectionable because it makes the 'finite infinite'.[4] What exactly does this mean? Certainly, according to the Jewish and Christian faiths, it has never been believed that the finite creature actually becomes God, whether before or after judgement. The idea of a final or ultimate judgement has rested on the conviction that a man may freely put himself, by his inner rebellion and consequent actions, into a position where he cannot any longer fit into the eternal realm ruled by the holy love of God. Here again, as we read further, it is not merely that Tillich is raising the question as to whether any man has sinned seriously enough to merit such exclusion from the divine presence. Nor is he only affirming his confidence, as Nels Ferré does, that the divine love must ultimately triumph over the most stubborn human heart and that, therefore, there will be at the end no permanent 'problem children in God's universe'. Certainly Tillich dislikes the idea of eternal punishment in its traditional form, and many who are not Tillichian may sympathize with him on that point.

[1] P. Tillich, *Systematic Theology*, vol. iii, p. 411.
[2] ibid., p. 400.
[3] ibid., p. 401.
[4] ibid., p. 407.

He rightly points out that there is an ambiguity about all human goodness and that 'even the saint remains a sinner and needs forgiveness and even the sinner is a saint in so far as he stands under the divine forgiveness'.[1] If Tillich was only saying that our acceptance by God does not depend upon our ethical and spiritual perfection but upon the forgiving mercy and compassion of God, much could be said in its favour. There is, however, more to it than that. 'The background of the imagery of a two-fold eternal destiny lies in the radical separation of person from person and of the personal from the sub-personal as a consequence of biblical personalism.'[2] It is this radical separation of person from person to which Tillich seems to be really objecting. And there can be no doubt that this is involved in the Christian view.

The fact that to become a person in the full sense demands a community of persons is not in question. Nor do we deny the physical, biological, psychological structures which constitute the context in and from which the individual person emerges. We agree, too, that the Christian does not think of his salvation as that of an isolated, atomic monad. To be saved in the Christian sense demands a community in which such terms as love and forgiveness and fellowship can have real significance. Christian love, however, demands the radical distinction of persons as alone making possible this profound sense of communion. This is why Tillich's term 'participation' is so ambiguous. Love which involved the complete destruction of the individuality of the two lovers would destroy itself as love, at least in the Christian sense of that word. Christian love yearns, not for identity in this sense, but for true communion.[3] Tillich's real sympathies seem to lie with that kind of mysticism in which individuality is not only transcended in a deeper experience of communion but which is completely transcended, indeed lost. This is why he is antipathetic to any idea of the continuation of the temporal life of the individual after death, with or without a body. The word temporal here is not only used in disparagement of any suggestion that the conditions of the next life will be similar to those in this life. Temporal here points to the radical separation of persons as individuals who can never be completely merged in the other. Hence the next life cannot be temporal in any sense whatsoever, because this would mean that individual persons would continue to exist after death and it is this latter point which Tillich appears to want to contest.

---

[1] P. Tillich, *Systematic Theology*, vol. iii, p. 408. [2] ibid., p. 407.
[3] R. George, *Communion with God*, p. 255.

The above critical comments might seem at first glance to be completely contradicted by what Tillich says on pages 413–4 of Volume III. There he says that 'the self-conscious self cannot be excluded from Eternal Life'.[1] But having said that, he then insists that the negation of this must be expressed with equal strength. We must be allowed to quote him again: 'As the participation of bodily being in Eternal life is not the endless continuation of a constellation of old or new physical particles, so the participation of the centered self is not the endless continuation of a particular stream of consciousness in memory and anticipation.'[2] Again: 'eternity transcends temporality and with it the experienced character of self-consciousness.'[3]

A similar ambiguity about survival is to be found in the writings of Bishop I. T. Ramsey. He too is concerned to make the point that the language of immortality involves a reference to a reality which is trans-temporal, in some sense beyond time. He rightly sees that to talk of the 'soul' or 'self' going on and on in a temporal chronological sense would not necessarily in itself point to this 'eternal' life as the experience of that which transcends the temporal. It is just possible that 'selves' might continue to exist after death, but without that qualitative experience of eternal life which will link the finite creature to God. It seems odd to the Western mind, deeply influenced by Christian ideas even when it repudiates the Christian faith, to talk of the survival of souls or selves in an after-life from which God is absent. Such a view was, however, defended by the philosopher McTaggart some years ago.[4] It is also found in some forms of Hindusim.[5] 'As there are many conscious beings in the world, the Samkhya adopts the view of the plurality of selves, both in the condition of bondage and of release.'[6] It is obviously possible to assert the continued existence of selves after death without believing in God in the Christian sense. The qualitative change, however, is implied in the Hindu Samkhya since the self (*purusa*) is liberated from its bondage to the unconscious *prakriti* (matter).

The case of Buddhism is more complex, since it has first to be decided whether nirvana can be interpreted to mean the survival of self-conscious persons. Professor Ninian Smart gives it as his opinion that 'in terms of the Buddha's metaphysics, it is wrong to say that the individual, even the Buddha himself, exists in nirvana.'[7] On the other

---

[1] P. Tillich, *Systematic Theology*, vol. iii, p. 413.   [2] ibid., p. 414.
[3] ibid., p. 414.   [4] J. M. E. McTaggart, *Some Dogmas of Religion*.
[5] N. Smart, *The Religious Experience of Mankind*, pp. 71 ff.
[6] S. Radhakrishnan and C. A. Moore, *A Source Book in Indian Philosophy*, p. 425.
[7] N. Smart, *The Religious Experience of Mankind*, p. 83.

side, Professor U. Thittala maintains that we must not be misled by the negative form of the terms (Pali *Nibbana* = the absence of craving: Sanskrit *nirvana* = the blowing out). 'The predominance of the negative explanation of Nibbana resulted in the mistaken notion that it is nothingness or annihilation.'[1]

In the Western context, Dr Ramsey also sees quite clearly that to talk of the self as merely going on and on does not yield a doctrine of immortality which would express what a Christian wants to signify by this term. 'Immortality' must stand for some kind of experience which we can have here and now that we are in touch with a reality which can never be described in space-time forms or about which we can use the language appropriate to our apprehension of 'objects' in this world. Where do we experience such a trans-temporal relationship? Primarily, says Dr Ramsey, when we make decisions which involve the acceptance of moral claims: 'to discover our duty is to discover our immortality, and vice-versa.'[2] This is not far removed from Tillich's position except that, for the latter, the quality of eternal life now experienced has a more than moral connotation. For both these writers, immortality designates a present quality of experience which links us to the trans-temporal reality, let us for the moment say God. The ordinary man will certainly be puzzled by this identification of immortality with the present discernment of his duty. For him, the word immortality still suggests some kind of existence after death, even when it is insisted that this involves not a mere going on and on but a new quality of existence. Is the plain man completely mistaken in this? It seems to me that Professor Lewis is right in his contention that one could accept all that Dr Ramsey says about the self and moral experiences and still be quite agnostic about our survival of death. 'We cannot conclude because we are persons and responsible beings that we are ipso facto immortal.'[3] To establish the latter conviction, we must go further than experiences which convince us that we are 'more than our observable behaviour'. If this is so, then other aspects of the Christian gospel need to be given greater weight, as we have ourselves maintained.

A similar ambiguity is to be found in David Edwards's recent book.[4] He asks whether it is a less worthy conception of immortality to be remembered by God than to survive in the manner claimed by spiri-

[1] K. W. Morgan (ed.), *The Path of the Buddha*, p. 112.
[2] I. T. Ramsey, *Freedom and Immortality*, p. 76.
[3] H. D. Lewis, *Freedom and History*, p. 310.
[4] D. L. Edwards, *Religion and Change*, p. 361

tualists. This, however, is surely to present us with a false 'either-or'. The implication seems to be that either we believe that the next life is an exact duplication of the present one, including its unworthy trivialities, or we must abandon any possibility of survival as self-conscious persons. Putting aside for the moment the question as to whether all spiritualists conceive of survival as sheer continuance divorced from quality of existence, it must be said that Christians on the whole have not conceived of life after death as 'history going on for ever and ever'. Much would depend upon what is meant by 'history' in this context. What seems to be left out of the picture is the possibility of the real transformation of individual persons by virtue of the fact that they are 'in Christ'. If the grace of God is operative in this transforming sense both in this life and the next, then it is not sufficient to talk of the next life as history going on for ever and ever. Certainly, inasmuch as the next life involves a community of persons, then one might perhaps speak of their history. Since, however, the word history suggests to most people the human drama of sin and imperfection in this world, we need another term to indicate the Christian hope of a community of just men made perfect through the transforming love of God in Christ. Therefore the hope of the life beyond is a 'going on' but not a mere 'going on'. To eliminate completely all temporal language about a 'going on' is, however, very difficult to do without giving the impression that persons do not survive as persons in the next life. Yet to roundly deny the latter possibility is to remove an important element of New Testament teaching and of the belief of the great majority of Christians from the beginning of the faith until now.

To return to Tillich in the light of this digression: one may well ask whether we can talk intelligibly of the real being or existence of persons after death if 'the experienced character of self-consciousness' is completely transcended as in Tillich's understanding of eternal life. It is hardly possible in this brief treatment to enter into a discussion of all the complex philosophical and psychological issues which this question raises. Several comments, however, can be made which may enable the reader to realize that there is another side to the story. Let it be repeated again that the Christian is committed on the basis of his faith in Christ, His teaching and His resurrection from the dead to the view that persons survive death as distinct individuals. Their annihilation or their complete absorption into 'God' cannot find support in any version of the complete faith which still remains loyal to the apostolic witness to Jesus Christ. The point at issue here is whether the New Testament could be cited in defence of the view that believers are annihilated at death. Whether God could or would permit the permanently impenitent, if such there be, to pass out of existence must be discussed later on its merits. Conditional immortality has had, as is well known, some notable defenders. We are simply contending here for the view that the annihilation of believers at death, as distinct from a temporary 'sleep', is not a view which can plausibly appeal to the New Testament for its justification.

We may concede to the critics at once that, whatever difficulties we may have in conceiving the meaning of space and time in a realm radically different from that of our present existence, it is not self-evident that space and time could have no meaning at all for persons after death. That God Himself is beyond space and time does not necessarily involve that finite persons must be beyond space and time in any and every form. Christians do not believe that persons after death literally become God. If the radical separation of persons continues after death, then it would seem to follow that such distinctness of persons requires that even after, some space-time framework is required to make such distinctness possible and intelligible.

Some years ago the late Canon Streeter wrote an essay on the resurrection of the body which still merits attention and consideration.[1] There he argues that space and time may be subjective for God but objective for us. If the relation of Creator and creature remains a reality after death and if perception implies a centre of consciousness at a particular point of space, asks Streeter, why should this not hold for the future life? We may have to admit our complete agnosticism about the exact nature of our experience of being persons after death. We have no imaginative symbols which would enable us to give a literal description of such an existence. Nevertheless, we may be justified in affirming the reality of such an individual existence if God is as Christians believe Him to be. Furthermore, space and time are not merely limitations which have to be shed. Space is a limitation for us now, because it often results in spiritual separation and as the frequent occasion of the frustration of our desires. Time is a limitation because it is bound up in our present experience with the failure to achieve our purposes and therefore with the problems of sin, guilt and the threat of death. These limitations could be overcome without our being taken completely and altogether out of some space-time framework which would be necessary to our continued existence as real and distinct individuals, however profound our communion with

[1] B. H. Streeter (ed.), *Immortality*.

each other through the indwelling of the divine love in us. Austin Farrer also remarks that there is no God-space in which other things than God can be lodged. Yet he does insist that 'Heaven is a created sphere where God bestows His presence by His action, especially His action through heart and mind.'[1] If, however, heaven is a created sphere, then the distinctions between Creator and creature and creature and creature must remain real and significant, however profound the communion of love may be. In order to avoid incautious talk about a heaven which could be reached by an astronaut, must we refuse to use all spatial and temporal symbols of the 'created order' of heaven?

The problem, however, still presents itself of finding appropriate symbols, images or 'myths' which would give at least some content to our understanding of what a 'next life' would be like. We shall concentrate here for a little upon the way in which Professor H. H. Price develops this theme, since it bears very closely upon our frequent reference to the question as to whether we should continue to use the language of resurrection or immortality. If the negative method is applied in this area, and we concentrate exclusively on saying what the next life is not, then all that is left is a mental blank. Naturally, such a view will neither satisfy the mind nor be a source of hope and inspiration. There is good reason to believe that this is in fact the position of many contemporary Christians. They have an uneasy feeling that the traditional symbols and images of the after-life are no longer adequate. On the other hand, they have not succeeded in replacing them. The result is a debilitating vagueness which has led to indifference to the whole question. The words of Canon Streeter are still applicable: 'Traditional pictures of hell are morally revolting; while the heaven of Sunday school teaching or popular hymnology is a place which the plain man does not believe to exist and which he would not want to go to if it did.'[2]

On the other hand, as Professor Price has recently insisted:[3] 'The idea of life after death is indeed a completely empty one unless we can form some rough conception of what the "other world" might be like.'[4] He suggests that we have a choice of developing two basic analogies. One starts from the assumption that personality cannot exist without a body of some kind. Since, as he admits, literal resuscitation has been rejected, we would have to postulate a 'higher' body on

---

[1] A. Farrer, *Saving Belief*, p. 144. [2] Streeter, op. cit., p. 135.
[3] A. Toynbee (ed.), *Man's Concern with Death* (see H. H. Price, 'What kind of next world?'). [4] ibid., p. 251.

97

which the self would depend in the next world. The next world, according to this view, would be a kind of 'material' world, and space and time in some sense would be meaningful in this new environment. This does not mean that the 'matter' of the next world would be manifest in the form to which the present laws of physics would apply. Nor do we have to assume that the 'space' we now experience is the only kind of space. 'There might perfectly well be two worlds, each standing in no spatial relationship to the other, or indeed, there might be more than two.'[1]

As opposed to this view, we might develop what he calls the 'disembodied' conception of survival. On this view, the self, soul, or spirit survives death without a body of any kind, retaining, however, consciousness, thought, memory, desire and the capacity to have emotions. On this view, many questions arise as to how we could retain our self-identity and self-awareness without a body, how we could experience that deepest of all bonds between persons, namely love. We might, suggests Price, think of the environment of the other world as a kind of dream world. To the objection that this makes the whole idea unreal or a phantasy, he replies that this may not be so. Mental imagery might play in the next world the role which sense-perception plays in this one. It might be every bit as detailed and vivid. It might include a body-image as in dreams in this life. Memories and desires would be preserved in the flow of mental images. It would be a psychological rather than a physical world. But on what grounds could one assert that the former is less 'real'? And as far as communication between selves is concerned, a highly developed form of telepathy would solve the problem.

In the light of our previous discussion, I think it could be said that the first view (Price's conception of 'embodied' survival) would fit more easily into the Hebrew concept of the whole man and the Christian retention of the concept of the resurrection of the body. The 'disembodied' version, however, making use of the immortality of the soul, has been widely influential also in Christian thought. Price's final conclusion is that the two views are not as far apart as may seem to be the case at first sight, and that we have to stretch the analogies to make them suitable, from whichever point we start. Our own view is that on this matter of being with or without a body, there is room for differing views within a context which is still Christian. Much depends upon the language we use and what we mean by it. We have to admit that we do not know for certain whether

[1] A. Toynbee (ed.), *Man's Concern with Death*, p. 253.

the 'self' can exist without a body of any kind. This would involve scientific and philosophical knowledge which modesty compels us to admit we do not at present have. Our line of argument certainly implies that we do not simply identify the 'self' with a body as such, whether physical or 'spiritual'. The 'self' is still more than the body, even if the latter is a *soma pneumatikon*. We accept H. D. Lewis's contention that the self is not the body, however closely related it may be to it.

No doubt the strongest reasons for retaining the language of resurrection are historical and theological. It is very difficult now, whatever our wishes, to state the immortality position in a way which does not seem to imply that man has a part of him which is intrinsically or by nature immortal. This, as we have seen, is not the biblical teaching. Helmut Thielicke makes much of this point, and it is his basis for the radical criticism of all use of immortality language.[1] For similar reasons, Farrer writes: 'It is better then to talk about the resurrection of man than about the immortality of the soul. Belief in resurrection is belief not in ourselves but in God who raises us. It is in fact the acid test.'[2] The reason for this emphasis is a concern, which is truly biblical, that man's basic confidence in a possible life after death is in God and not in the conviction that man, whether in whole or in part, is immortal in the sense of being incapable of passing out of existence. If we do continue to live after death, it is because God wills it and because it is His loving intention to bring it about for us, as He did in the raising of His Son from the dead. The semantic problem remains, and it is difficult to see how agreement upon a common and consistent vocabulary is to be brought about. As we have seen, immortality language and resurrection language can both be made to bear the meaning which a Christian would want to give to it in the light of his understanding of God. Also both kinds of language can be used in a way which he would want to repudiate, namely that man is intrinsically immortal or that the resurrection life involves the possession of the present physical body in the exact form in which he now has it. There seems to be no solution to this language problem except the careful education of Christian people in a proper understanding of what their faith implies. At the very least, we cannot abandon the Christian hope that we exist after death as real persons, that we have communion with God and with each other without losing our individuality, and that our relationship with God

---

[1] H. Thielicke, *Death and Life*.
[2] A. Farrer, *Saving Belief*, p. 141.

and one another depends upon the basic fact of being 'in Christ'. If we are assured of these truths, then we can be content to be agnostic about details, provided the agnosticism is not total, for in that case the Christian hope has evaporated and we are of all men most to be pitied.

Chapter Seven

Hell and Judgement

This chapter will prepare the way for a discussion of heaven, but since modern man's difficulties with the notion of heaven spring from its connection with other associated ideas, we shall deal with these latter first. Let us, however, make a brief summary of the stages of our argument so far.

It has been contended that the fact and meaning of death are the most neglected aspects of modern thought, not only in humanist and secular circles but very often in presentations of the Christian faith. As a reaction against a false and one-sided other-worldliness, this has some real justification. Carried to the extreme of a radical and exclusive this-worldliness, it is a mutilation of the whole gospel. The abandonment of the eternal hope, in the sense of the survival of individuals after death into a worthwhile existence, is really the destruction of hope. However much men concentrate upon the transformation of this world, this hope of a better order here and now cannot be a satisfactory substitute for the confidence of the individual's preservation after death into the kingdom of God where death no longer reigns. To interpret eternal life as a new quality of existence here and now, however true and important, is only half of the story. God, for Christians, does not care only for quality of life in the abstract. He cares for individual persons, and their final destiny is His supreme concern. It has been shown that this is in conformity with the teaching of Jesus. He did speak of the survival of individuals after death into the resurrection mode of existence. He did not view this, however, as simply the continuance of the physical body in its present form. Yet he did not deny the Jewish idea of the existence of the individual after death in a 'body' of some kind.

We then digressed to deal with certain objections to this view made in the name of science and philosophy. It was shown that neither of these compels us to treat man as only his body and no more. Contrary to what many believe, the reality of the self or mind or spirit or soul as distinct from the body can still be asserted by men who are fully acquainted with science and philosophy. The 'self' is not reducible to physical process without remainder. The body-mind issue and the problem of self-identity cannot be dismissed as bogus questions which can be ignored on the mistaken assumption that science and philosophy have rendered a negative verdict certain. The survival of the individual after death can, therefore, be discussed with an open mind in the light of the positive insights which the Christian faith brings to bear upon this issue. It has been frankly admitted that for the Christian, the question cannot be resolved on a purely empirical basis in the narrow sense of this word. There is, of course, no reason why the word empirical should be monopolized by those who stand in the tradition of Hume and his successors.[1] His confidence in going beyond the cautious statements of science and philosophy depends upon his conviction about the character and reality of God and the centrality of Christ for a proper understanding of God. This is not an appeal to wishful thinking, since the Christian view of God is itself based upon certain types of evidence given in experience and is, therefore, in a broad sense empirically based. The Christian cannot and must not accept the criteria of the physical senses as the sole test of truth and reality, for this is precisely the issue.

In this chapter, then, we shall assume that the Christian faith, the person of Christ, the philosophical handling of the problem of the 'self', the proper evaluation of the mind-body issue, all give the Christian reasonable grounds for affirming confidently the survival of the individual after death. Whether the survival is in some sense an 'embodied' existence and what 'body' means in this context is, as already noticed, a difficult question. It is not resolved by a simple appeal to Hebrew as against Greek thought. Whatever may be said for Hebrew anthropology, it is impossible for modern thought to equate resurrection with resuscitation of the identical body of earth. Even if some kind of body is the organ of the self after death as before death, it is still impossible to identify the self which exists after death completely and wholly with the body, even if with a 'spiritual' body, whatever this may precisely signify.

To rescue this belief in the survival of death from the limitations of a merely abstract idea, however, it has to be clothed in images and symbols which express the truth in a manner which stirs the imagination and becomes a source of positive joy and hope in the daily living of the Christian life in this world. In the course of Christian

---

[1] For a reasoned defence of a broader definition of empirical cf. J. E. Smith, *Reason and God.*

history, however, the positive hope of eternal life beyond death has been closely linked with other doctrines, in particular that of hell and eternal punishment. So much is this the case that it is often asserted that fear of hell has been a far more potent factor in the lives of men than the hope of heaven. Nor can it be denied that in certain periods of history, and for certain individuals in widely separated epochs, this has been in large measure true. This has led critics of many different kinds to question the justice of any such Christian hope, whether positive or negative. Assuming that the belief in personal immortality or some reinterpreted form of resurrection existence is part of Christian faith, does this mean that only Christians can qualify? What of the millions who lived before Christ and never heard the word of the gospel? What of those in the Christian era who are in like ignorance by virtue of being nurtured in another faith, such as Hinduism, Buddhism or Islam? Furthermore, what man of sensitive conscience and compassion would really want to receive eternal life from a God who is content to assign the vast majority of the human race to eternal punishment in a hell where suffering is purely retributive, and by definition can have no value either as purifying or in the sense of rehabilitation? There can be no doubt that these latter views can be and are a powerful inhibiting factor, for many assume that the hope of heaven cannot be separated from the opposite negative view.

We shall therefore examine first the traditional doctrine of hell with a view to showing that the positive does not necessarily depend upon the negative, at least as the negative has been traditionally understood. It goes without saying that the Christian is committed by the very nature of his faith to take with the utmost seriousness the moral or spiritual decision or decisions by which he responds to the word of the gospel: 'Repent, for the kingdom of heaven is at hand'. Neither heredity nor physical and psychological factors nor the pressure of the social environment can fully destroy the responsibility of man to accept God's invitation or not. They may mitigate the degree of the responsibility and the Christian must believe that God will take such circumstances into account. Furthermore, what a man does with his life in this world is of great consequence, not only for earthly existence but for what which awaits him after death. Moral and spiritual decisions, which shape character now, also have eternal consequences. This remains true whatever answer is given to the question as to whether physical death is the point of final judgement. Such issues as this will be considered later. The doctrine of hell, whatever its other defects, still expresses the importance of present spiritual decisions and loyalties for the eternal destiny of men, eternal here meaning not only present quality of life but some kind of real existence after death.

Having said this, however, it has to be admitted that in no area of Christian thought is it more easy for sub-Christian ideas to influence our thinking. Enemies of Christianity have not been slow to charge that Christians have often reserved hell for their enemies and remained strangely silent about the gospel injunction to love our enemies. As Cyril Emmet observed: 'The growth of the belief in hell was largely due to a very intelligible indignation at the cruelty of persecutors and a desire to stem heresy.[1]' We can understand why Tertullian reacted as he did without necessarily giving our moral approval.[2] When modern men condemn so vigorously the hatred of Christians for those who inflict upon them such unspeakable tortures and sufferings, they often forget the modern manifestations of hate. We have only to remember the utter hatred and loathing which have been expressed in our day for Nazis and Communists and by the latter for Christians and by Christians for Communists. Those involved in racial tensions and civil rights protests and defenders of good causes in our time have not been slow to use the most vitriolic language about their opponents and enemies. We are not contending that two blacks make a white and that because modern men hate so well, then it is quite permissible for Christians to do the same with a clear conscience. There is, however, a rather nauseating hypocrisy about moral indignation against the doctrine of hell while claiming at the same time freedom to hate, kill and torture in the name of political and social utopias on earth. If hatred or the desire for the destruction of our enemies is wrong for Christians, it is wrong as such. Nor is it sufficient to reply that for the Christian it is far worse because he believes in a God of love. Most of our modern horrors have been committed in the name of high-sounding moral ideals, whether it be the classless state, social justice, freedom and equality, patriotism or what have you.

We shall return now for a time to the calmer atmosphere of historical study before confronting again the agonizing problems of moral approval or disapproval. It is sometimes argued that, although the doctrines of hell and of eternal punishment are terrible doctrines, they must be accepted by the Christian because they represent the plain teaching of Jesus Christ and have behind them His authority, plus that of the Bible and the Church. To question them, therefore,

[1] B. H. Streeter (ed.), *Immortality*, p. 204.
[2] Tertullian, *De Spectaculis*, 30.

is to question all these authorities and, therefore, to cease to be in any recognizable sense a Christian. Now it may be admitted that modern secular men do not attach much importance to authorities, and some radical theologians would agree with them on this point. This, however, is a difficult position for the ordinary Christian to occupy. He still feels that in confessing that Jesus is Lord, he is committed to accepting substantially His teaching as far as we can discern what this is. If the doctrine of hell in the sense of eternal punishment was a clear and unambiguous part of His teaching, then he would be faced with the difficult decision either of accepting it on authority alone or rejecting it and deciding on his own moral authority that Jesus was wrong on this important issue. We may be forced into this latter view after careful study, but we have no right to assume that this is the only option before us. It is possible that Jesus had a doctrine of hell, but not of eternal punishment. It is this thesis which it is proposed to examine. To those who insist that the two cannot be separated, we can only plead for a suspense of judgement until our study is complete.

In terms of our previous discussion of personal survival of death, it is important to define clearly what eternal punishment would mean in this context. It does not mean simply a state of present human existence, though some kind of hell on earth is obviously not an impossibility. The traditional form of the doctrine has insisted that those who have rejected God and been rejected by Him will continue to exist after death 'forever'. Furthermore, they will suffer for 'unlimited time' pains and sufferings which are purely retributive, that is they are punishments, and are justified because such people deserve to be punished. They are not purifying sufferings, as in the Roman Catholic purgatory. Nor are they disciplinary sufferings whose purpose is to rehabilitate the sinner, as some of our modern liberal reformers of the penal code would insist. Hell by definition is endless, retributive punishment and the sinner exists for ever in this state of penal suffering. There is no need at this stage to discuss how literally the pains of hell are to be interpreted. Whether they are symbolic of mental and psychological anguish or involve something very similar to bodily pain, the basic point is the same. The sinner exists for ever in a state of excruciating and endless suffering. The question we shall try to answer is whether this is the plain and unambiguous teaching of Jesus as this can be found in the gospel sources.

One of the fundamental difficulties in dealing with this kind of question springs from deep differences of opinion as to how the biblical sources should be interpreted, particularly the gospels. Those who hold a verbal inspiration theory of Scripture regard the gospels as authoritative *per se*, which often means when read in a quite uncritical and undiscriminating way. They reject any attempt to analyse the sources of the gospels, and therefore do no leave open the possibility of the influence of contemporary ideas, whether Jewish or Gentile or of later Church tradition. This means that, in practice, all statements bearing upon the subject of hell, wherever found in the New Testament must be of equal truth and validity. One then proceeds to collect all the relevant references and seek to harmonize them in some eschatological pattern. This may and often does involve a good deal of artificial forcing of the data to make them fit the pattern which the person in question has decided *is* the biblical pattern.

A good example of this is the subject of the millennium. There is, for example, no specific mention of the millennium in any of the gospel sources. There is a reference, however, to it in Revelation 20: 1–6. On the basis of this single definite reference in the New Testament, it is assumed that some form of millennial doctrine must constitute an essential element in any possible eschatological pattern. The various gospel passages dealing with eschatological matters are then fitted into this framework, despite the fact that we have no reason to think that the millennial idea played any significant part in the thought of Jesus, if the evidence of the gospels is treated as our basic source. This assumption or manner of procedure is in our view questionable. It is not *a priori* certain that the whole of the New Testament must have a completely consistent eschatological pattern. This does not mean that there may not be basic recurring themes and similar attitudes. Yet we cannot rule out in advance the possibility that the early Christian communities were influenced by ideas not wholly consistent with what the Master taught.

The alternative to a perfectly consistent scheme of eschatology is not, on the other hand, sheer chaos or a total scepticism about the gospels. The literary and historical material must be examined on its merits. As a matter of principle, however, if there is a real and basic clash between the 'mind' of Christ as disclosed in the gospels and what is found in the other New Testament writings and later tradition, the preference must be given to the gospels. The reason for this is that the gospels remain the only and classic source of what Jesus thought about any topic whatsoever. A total scepticism about the gospels would, of course, render useless any attempt to discern the thought of Jesus, not only in regard to hell, but also in regard to

God, the kingdom of God, grace, forgiveness, moral principles, or even the supremacy of agape-love about which we hear so much today. Such radical scepticism is in our view unjustified.[1] We believe that the gospels can and should be studied without the distorting bias of a complete scepticism. This does not mean uncritically, but it does mean a study in which the fullest possible critical awareness of our own presuppositions is also involved. It is not suggested that historical research leads inevitably to the spiritual judgement expressed in the confession that Jesus is Lord. On the other hand, it is not implied that faith can dispense with any and all historical assurance based on a study of the documents by methods which the professional historian would acknowledge as valid. Nor in concentrating upon the gospels do we necessarily imply a complete dichotomy between the so-called Jesus of history and the Christ of faith. These large theological issues must be discussed on their merits, and they cannot be dealt with adequately now. All that is being claimed is that the study of the gospels, in order to discover what Jesus thought, is not a hopeless undertaking doomed to frustration from the start.[2]

We shall now concentrate upon what the gospels have to say about hell, eternal life and eternal punishment. The average man or the simple believer is apt to be impatient with the careful and scholarly study of the biblical language. He has only read the Bible in his native tongue, say English. He comes across the word 'eternal' and assumes without question that this means endless time. No further questions need be asked. He comes across the word 'hell' and he knows that many Christians have believed this to involve eternal punishment. This ends the matter of interpretation as far as he is concerned. Any attempt to penetrate behind these assumptions and find out if the original biblical languages plainly suggest this interpretation, is regarded as open or hidden modernism devoted to the destruction of the gospel and the authority of Scripture. This attitude cannot be justified. If Scripture is held to contain divine truth, then every legitimate linguistic, literary and historical tool must be used in order to gain the assurance that we have truly understood what in fact Scripture says. On no subject is this more important than in regard to our chosen themes of hell and eternal punishment.

On any analysis of the gospels, it is difficult to avoid the conclusion that Jesus did sometimes use the word 'Gehenna'. This word, translated 'hell', occurs eighteen times in the Authorized Version, five as

[1] A. T. Hanson (ed.), *Vindications*.
[2] T. W. Manson, *Studies in the Gospels and Epistles*, Chs. 1–7.

a translation of Hades, twelve of Gehenna and once of another lesser-known Greek word for the abode of the dead (Tartaros) in 2 Peter 2: 4. The references to Gehenna are those most relevant to our immediate theme. The crucial question therefore, concerns the interpretation and the exact meaning of Gehenna on the lips of Jesus. Even if we accept the view that Matthew does some touching up and heightening of this kind of language, the gospel sources as a whole point strongly to at least some occasions when Jesus used the word. What did He mean by it and intend us to understand by it? How do we go about finding an answer to this kind of question. It cannot be assumed that Jesus' use of Gehenna in itself solves the problem of whether He taught eternal punishment. It is precisely the significance and meaning of the word which is under debate. The following basic questions arise to which some kind of an answer has to be given before any further judgement on this issue can be made.

(1) Was the term Gehenna used in the Judaism of His day and what did it mean in that context?

(2) Assuming that the meaning or meanings of Gehenna in the Judaism of the period can be determined, have we any grounds for thinking that Jesus simply took over such contemporary ideas without modification or did He retain the term and give it a new or modified meaning?

(3) Did Jesus take for granted the inevitable survival of death for believers and unbelievers into a resurrection mode of existence which was eternal in the sense of never coming to an end? If He did and at the same time held the view that some are punished after death, then logically the doctrine of eternal punishment would follow unless one could show that Jesus held such punishment to be remedial only and was, therefore, committed to the view that all men would in the end be saved. Another aspect of this same issue is whether Jesus held any view of the intrinsic immortality of the soul. If so, then the soul could not be destroyed after death, and some doctrine of eternal punishment would follow, or universal salvation as indicated above.

(4) Another possibility is that Jesus did not believe in the survival of death at all, and that He was only interested in the quality of human existence here and now. In this case, if He did say anything about heaven or hell, it would refer only to man's state in this world. Gehenna would then describe man's separation from God here and now in this present life. In so far as this involved punishment now in the form of psychological or physical suffering or both, hell would designate this present state of man in his rebellion against God. Hell

would be the reaping of what He has sown and the painful consequences of this in the present life, plus the spiritual anguish of knowing that God had rejected him. Death, however, would be the end for the individual and, therefore, of his heaven or hell as the case may be. Without denying the concern of Jesus for the state of men in this life, we have already argued in a previous chapter that it is highly unlikely that Jesus was so radically this-worldly as to deny the survival of death by individual persons. This seems highly improbable in view of the Judaism in which He was nurtured and what we learn from the gospels. For this reason, therefore, we shall concentrate on the first three questions raised, which are the crucial ones.

First—was the term Gehenna used in the Judaism of Jesus' day and what did it mean in that context? It has often been pointed out by biblical scholars that Judaism was late in developing a doctrine of the resurrection, whether to life and bliss or to punishment for the wicked. We may agree with Neville Clark that Old Testament thought is 'expressive of a passionate unveiling of the heights and depths of fellowship with God, which is already implicitly undermining the finality of death.'[1] The full implications of this were only to be unfolded after a simple theology of rewards and punishments in this life had broken down under the pressure of experience. If God's justice and righteousness were truly to be vindicated, this could only be affirmed if Sheol, the abode of the dead, could somehow be brought under the control and jurisdiction of Yahweh. It is this that we see happening in the period between the Old Testament and the New in the so-called apocalyptic and apocryphal writings. In these, we see a radical change of thought about individual destiny after death. Three characteristics can be discerned.[2]

(i) The dead are no longer 'shades' in whom life has been reduced almost to vanishing point. They are spoken of as souls or spirits and survive as individual conscious beings. Whereas for Old Testament thought personality was wholly dependent on the body, now in some measure at least the continued existence of the discarnate soul in separation from the body could be conceived.

(ii) Moral obligations appear in Sheol. There the good and bad receive their deserts.

(iii) Sheol is divided up into several compartments according to the moral and spiritual condition of the souls which go there.

Now it could be argued that these later developments of Judaism

[1] N. Clark, *Interpreting the Resurrection*, p. 20.
[2] D. Russell, *The Method and Message of Jewish Apocalyptic*.

form a classical escape from realities or an exercise in misguided wish-fulfilment, the bringing in of another world to redress the balance of the present one. It was a form of psychological compensation generated by the intolerable pressures of national disaster and individual suffering. On the other hand, it could be maintained that it was only the complete unfolding of the logic inherent in the Old Testament faith in God—His sovereignty, holiness, love and lordship over history. Which of these versions we adopt cannot be decided only on historical and exegetical grounds. It will depend upon the truth which we believe to belong to the biblical understanding of God and its culmintion in Christianity. Because it is a fact that there is much fantasy in the writings of the inter-testamentary period, and motives of revenge and vindictiveness which the Christian cannot countenance, it is unreasonable to dismiss this whole development of thought as if it were wholly an illusory and perverted compensation. We have to recognize none the less that it is not possible from this literature to derive a perfectly consistent scheme of thought. On the following basic issues, there are differing views.

(a) Is death the point of final judgement? Dr Russell is of the opinion that 'no moral change is possible once men have departed this life'.[1] 1 Enoch 62:2 and 2 Baruch 85:12 may be cited as illustrative of this position.

(b) Resurrection and judgement at the end of the age, that is when history reaches its term, seems to be the general presupposition. There is no universal agreement that resurrection will necessarily be general. The wicked are sometimes raised at the end to be punished with the 'body'. Sometimes no need is seen for their resurrection at all. Physical death is their final end and judgement. Sheol-Gehenna is the final state of judgement for the wicked. Whether they are annihilated in Sheol is not always clear. In Jubilees Sheol is the place where the wicked are slain, but not necessarily annihilated, for it is a 'place from which they will never escape'. (103:7–8) In 1 Enoch 22:10–11, Sheol is a place of torment, though the actual word Gehenna is not used. Whether the wicked in Sheol have a 'body' of some kind is again not clear. Some Greek influence may be discernible but it is not decisive. Even if the apocalyptic literature can conceive of 'soul' without body where there is no suggestion of Greek influence, for the most part the 'soul' in Sheol has to be united again with the body at the general resurrection in order that the whole man may be judged and punished.

[1] D. Russell, *The Method and Message of Jewish Apocalyptic*, p. 155.

The difficult question we have to try and answer is where Jesus fits into this pattern of thought. Since there is not a uniform pattern but sometimes views which are mutually contradictory, we cannot conceive of Jesus taking over undigested and without discrimination the whole of apocalyptic. He must have made some selection of elements. The crucial question is: what elements did He select and what degree of emphasis and importance did He ascribe to such elements?

This brings us back to our second question. Did Jesus simply take over such contemporary ideas, or did He make His own selection and give the items selected a new or modified meaning? To answer this presupposes that we can arrive at a reasonably accurate knowledge of the main features of Jesus' own thinking. This presents its own problem in view of the fact that the New Testament writings do themselves reflect the influence of eschatological and apocalyptic ideas of Judaism just prior to the Christian era and during the first Christian century. It may therefore be argued that, for critical reasons, it is no longer possible to isolate the thinking of Jesus of Nazareth from the early Christian community's interpretation of His teaching and of the significance of His Person. In theory it is possible to make a distinction between the mind of Jesus and the contemporary eschatology and apocalyptic. In practice, it is argued, it is impossible to draw the distinction with accuracy because we cannot isolate the actual teaching of Jesus from all the later influences and interpretations. This leaves us with the New Testament material which unquestionably contains references to Gehenna, the Parousia and other such matters. However, we are no longer in a position to say whether the role played by these ideas in the New Testament documents as we have them really reflects the mind of Jesus of Nazareth. Failing this possibility, only the following options are open, We either accept the New Testament documents in their present form as authoritative, according to some theory of infallible inspiration, or we accept the authority of the Church in one of its traditional forms and therefore its interpretation of whatever historical core lies behind the documents.

In our view neither of these appeals to the infallibility of Book or Church or both is possible in this uncritical and undiscriminating form. This means that we must try to come with grips with the problem of gaining some knowledge of the mind of Jesus which can claim some reliable historical character, and which can be distinguished from the developing process of theological interpretation in the early days of the Church's history. This means that we must discover, if we can, what Jesus thought about God, since this is obviously crucial for any further discussion about such topics as eternal punishment. If, as we have contended, such questions cannot be answered simply on the grounds of general philosophical considerations, then a Christian treatment of the issue will have to depend upon whatever deductions it is proper to make from the character of God. This is not to deny that it might be possible to develop doctrines of immortality and even punishment after death on philosophical grounds or by appealing to non-Christian intuitions of the nature of the transcendent. Plato could obviously be cited as an example of the first, and the Hindu and Buddhist concepts of karma as an example of the second. How far we are convinced by such ideas will depend upon whether we accept the Platonic philosophy as giving us the truest insight into the nature of reality, or whether the Hindu and Buddhist world-views perform the same role in our thinking and understanding as to where the truth lies.

Let us concentrate for a moment upon the Christian faith, and ask how from the Christian perspective one would go about assessing the complex of ideas which appears in the period of late Judaism. Are there any ideas here which we could still claim as insights into the truth still valid for us and not simply interesting aspects of the religious history of a particular period no longer relevant to modern man? If the early faith of Israel in a holy, righteous and compassionate Creator-God was a valid insight into the nature and character of the reality on which man depends, then certain consequences would seem logically to follow. In this case it could be argued that the eschatological and apocalyptic developments of inter-testamentary Judaism were the attempt to draw out the implications of the previous faith of Israel. This does not mean that everything that was said was either valid or consistent, but it does leave open the possibility that some developments were legitimate and still valid provided the character of God as disclosed in the earlier history is also valid.[1] Assuming, then, that the basic insights into the reality and character of God were and are valid, then it is possible to see that certain deductions made by later Judaism were fundamentally in line with these insights.

For example, the clearer the conviction that God is a God of holy love, of covenant love (hesed), the more incredible it would become to conceive of Him as simply allowing His people to perish at death. The urge to extend the jurisdiction of Yahweh over the abode of

[1] For a very penetrating discussion of the rational grounds for belief in God in the Judaeo-Christian sense, see H. P. Owen, *The Christian Knowledge of God*.

the dead (Sheol) was a perfectly natural development from the character of God as previously known. The fact that it took many centuries and a long historical development before Judaism drew out these implications of its faith does not invalidate the point. To fix the essence of the Jewish faith at its very early stages and to refuse to consider its organic growth through later historical developments and experiences is surely an arbitrary proceeding. The appearances in later Judaism of doctrines of resurrection and immortality were not irrelevant addenda tacked on to a faith which did not need them. Rather they were simply giving expression to the view that God's power and love were supreme over death, and that after death, His people could rely on Him to sustain them in being, not simply for the sake of going on and on, but that they might enter fully into the bliss of a perfected fellowship with the God whom we know, at least in part, here and now. If this development was justified on the basis of Old Testament faith, how much more on the basis of the deepened assurance of the love of God the Father (Abba) in the life, death and resurrection of Jesus Christ. It is admitted, of course, that for those who for one reason or another cannot believe in God in this sense, the later deductions concerning life after death will carry little weight. All we are concerned to maintain for the moment is that if such a faith in God is valid, then the later developments in regard to death and victory over it were both natural and inevitable.

Secondly, if God is a God of holy love, where full weight is given to the holy as not only the numinous but the morally righteous, then life after death cannot be meaningfully detached from moral issues. Notions of righteousness, sin, disobedience, punishment, guilt, suffering all now become relevant. If God is righteous, then the bliss of fellowship with Him cannot be conceived in separation from all questions concerning man's reflection of that righteousness in his basic attitudes and actions, whether we are thinking of this life or the next. This holds good, whatever view is taken of such debatable questions as legalism and justification. That God does not deal with us simply as a Judge, following a rigid code of rewards and punishments, does not alter this fact. Even if God accepts us as we are, that is sinners, on the basis of faith in Christ, and does not make His forgiveness and mercy depend upon our already achieved goodness and perfection, this cannot mean that God is completely uninterested in the kind of men and women we can become 'in Christ'. He does not want us to remain eternal sinners but to be transformed into the likeness of His Son as we respond in freedom to His holy love. Life after death, therefore, will inevitably be related both to man's attitude of acceptance or rejection of God's love, and to what he can become when he submits in love and trust to God's love. Fellowship with God or separation from Him thus become decisive elements in any thought of life after death. They are, of course, decisive in this life also and therefore also decisive in any continued existence after death. When late Judaism made deductions concerning Yahweh's power over the realm of death and of the importance and reality of moral distinctions in Sheol, it was acting quite properly on the basis of its faith in God. The New Testament confirms and extends this process. It is true that the New Testament deepens the conviction of the possibility of a present foretaste of eternal life because the kingdom is already present in the Person and mission of Jesus and in the Spirit-endowed community which arose as a consequence. It never loses, however, the conviction that the kingdom in its fullness is still to come, and that the rule of God extends beyond death to the resurrection mode of life in which believers survive death.

To sum up, our conclusion is that Jesus Himself endorsed and confirmed the faith of Israel in its developed form. God is the loving, holy, righteous Creator-God who is also Father. The present rule of God inaugurated in His ministry is the prelude to the final rule of God which extends beyond death. Men survive death in a resurrection mode which is not the resuscitation of the present body, but is nevertheless real and genuine individual and personal existence. Loving acceptance or judgement involving rejection are real possibilities after death and when history comes to a close. This is not based on an arbitrary decree of God, but is rooted in the responsible freedom of men to accept their place in God's universe or to opt out of it.

So much it seems possible to say with a fair degree of assurance. The difficulties arise when it comes to details. We have already seen that there is no question of Jesus endorsing everything that was said in the eschatological and apocalyptic developments of the period which preceded His own appearance. The obvious reason for this is that much of this material contains conflicting views, some of which are so mutually contradictory that there is no possibility of reconciling them in any consistent pattern of thought. Jesus must have selected some elements and rejected others, unless we refuse to Him the power to recognize a contradiction when He saw it. There is, for example, no evidence that Jesus ever endorsed the idea of a divine victory over the enemies of Israel interpreted in the narrowest racial and nationalist sense. That the Jews would gain a bloody victory over their enemies and emerge as the victors with their heels on the necks of their foes is a vision of the future which plays no part in the expectations of Jesus. On the other hand, some of the apocalyptic images were employed by Jesus, including the term Gehenna. How are these images to be interpreted, and have we any reason to believe that when using Gehenna, Jesus meant by it, not only future judgement and separation from God, but the idea of eternal punishment, that is the everlasting reality of retributive punishment which by very definition is neither remedial nor deterrent only, but suffering inflicted on the basis of moral desert, and a suffering which can never come to an end by God's permitting the sufferer to pass out of existence altogether?

In the light of the somewhat lengthy discussion of Gehenna, we can now give a quick answer to our second question. Jesus, as we have seen, could not have taken over all the ideas associated with Gehenna in late Judaism and apocalyptic because they are mutually contradictory and in some cases impossible to reconcile with what Jesus tells us elsewhere about the character of God. Nevertheless, He did use the term and it appears to be connected with His understanding of the future kingdom, with the implication of grace and judgement for men according to their response or failure to respond to the divine invitation. The meaning of Gehenna, therefore, must be sought within this context of ideas. We are led then to our next series of questions.

We have already rejected the solution suggested in our fourth question, namely that Jesus had no interest in a life after death, and interpreted the symbols of heaven, Gehenna, etc. only in terms of states of existence in this world. Evidence has been adduced in support of the view that Jesus believed in personal immortality after death in an 'embodied' form, that is in some doctrine of resurrection. It was also noted that He rejected the idea of a resuscitation of the present physical body in an unchanged form. On the other hand, there is no reason to think that He was directly affected by the Greek dualism of body and soul and philosophical ideas of immortality. Our conclusion, then, is that Jesus starts with the assumption that man's eternal destiny is an existence after death under the rule of God and as a member of the community of all the redeemed. At the same time, final judgement is linked with the Parousia at the end of the present age. Since He appears to have worked with this idea of the two ages, the present age and the age to come, then it could be argued that 'aeonian' punishment refers not to a chronologically unlimited punishment but to the judgement of God at the end of the coming age. There is nothing to prevent the deduction that at the final judgement, the stubbornly impenitent will be allowed by God to pass out of existence, not because He desires this but because such people have declared their unwillingness to exist in the kind of world God has created. Whether any man will be finally impenitent in this sense is a question not to be dogmatically answered, as was evident in our previous discussion of the subject. We are dealing now not with the details but with the basic presuppositions which must govern any Christian understanding of God's attitude to men at the final judgement. Gehenna, therefore, stands for God's negative judgement at the End when their eternal separation from God is confirmed. The New Testament evidence is not plain enough to permit us to affirm that such separation involves the keeping of the impenitent alive for ever for the purpose of retributive punishment alone.

A final comment can be made here in regard to the charge previously considered that to separate the moment of physical death from final judgement is to weaken the urgency of repentance and the acceptance of the gospel. This in our view would only be true if the idea of a final judgement were to be eliminated altogether. That this was in fact the case in a good deal of nineteenth-century Protestant theology has been amply shown in a very incisive study of this period in a recent book.[1]

It seems appropriate at this point to add a brief comment on Ian Ramsey's chapter on hell in *Talk of God*. With his basic thesis we are in full sympathy and agreement. Our reservations arise when he uses such language as the following: 'Death would seem to be such a major spatio-temporal discontinuity, judging from what happens to the body at death, that there seems little reason to suppose that life after death is in a time series continuous with the present, or that it embodies spatial features which bear much resemblance to what we know now.'[2] In rightly stressing the radical discontinuity between life in the body here and now and any form of life after death, Dr Ramsey does seem to evade the question raised earlier by Professor Lewis as to the sense in which we can be said to 'be' or to 'exist' after death. Life after death may not be in a time series continuous with the present 'in any simple sense of time as measured by our clocks'. On the other hand, unless we are to opt for the reality of persons only in this present temporal-spatial form of existence, then, as we have previously

[1] J. P. Martin, *The Last Judgment in Protestant Theology from Orthodoxy to Ritschl.*

[2] I. T. Ramsey, 'Hell' in Royal Institute of Philosophy Lectures, vol. 2, 1967–8 *Talk of God*, p. 210.

argued, we may be compelled to use temporal and spatial symbols, however qualified, in order to point to a genuine existence of persons after death. It is obvious, of course, that Dr Ramsey's critique of hell for 'presupposing a life *after* death' would apply with equal force to any defence of heaven as involving the blessed existence of 'real persons' after death. It is not always clear how far he wishes to go in this respect. His attack upon everlasting retributive punishment as inconsistent with the Christian notion of God seems to us altogether convincing. Yet does it follow from this that the idea of a limited existence and punishment after death is inconsistent in the same way? In opting for the model of separation rather than punishment,[1] is Dr Ramsey not necessarily weakening the biblical ideas of holiness and judgement? Is not separation itself a kind of punishment if it means separation from the source of the fullest and truest human life? Should our fear of distorted sub-Christian and all too human ideas of punishment lead us to abandon altogether the idea of God's anger against sin and the suffering consequent upon man's rejection of God?[2] However, our chief dissatisfaction with Dr Ramsey's position at present concerns his lack of definiteness concerning the real existence of persons after death. In seeking to free the language of the after-life from a naive and uncritical use of spatial and temporal symbols, is he not in danger of emptying of all content the Christian hope of a real personal existence and fellowship with God after death? Whatever the risks involved, we have defended the use of such language as inevitable if the eternal reality of persons is to be preserved in a way which human thought and imagination can in part grasp.

It is also a fact that in much contemporary theology, the biblical realism in respect to final judgement at the end of history has either been eliminated or profoundly transformed in the direction of a Platonizing symbolism or an exclusively 'realized eschatology'. At the same time, the presuppositions of modern 'secular' man and some secularized versions of the Christian faith have completely lost the sense of a personal God working out His purpose through the historical order to a final goal or consummation. Coupled with a disregard of the biblical understanding of the holiness of God and of God's righteous reaction against sin, this has led to the almost complete disappearance from modern Western consciousness of the concepts of grace and judgement in relation to man's ultimate destiny. No wonder,

[1] I. T. Ramsey, 'Hell' in Royal Institute of Philosophy Lectures, vol. 2, 1967–8 *Talk of God*, p. 223.
[2] E. Bevan, *Symbolism and Belief*. See chapter on Wrath of God.

therefore, that if someone suggests that death is not the moment of final judgement, this seems to be a further weakening of moral and spiritual seriousness and an invitation to laxity. This is not, however, the position defended here. What we have to say on all these topics is said within the context of an interpretation of history as the arena for the purposive activity of the transcendent, holy and personal God who became man in Jesus Christ and who will bring His redemptive purpose to its consummation through Him who is still to come when this age reaches its term.

Let us sum up again the conclusions at which we have arrived.

(*a*) Any doctrine of hell must be consistent with the view of God as holy love, where holy love is to be interpreted in the light of its manifestation in the life, ministry, death and resurrection of Jesus Christ.

(*b*) There will be a real existence of persons of an 'embodied' kind after death. This does not involve the view that man as such has an element in his nature which is intrinsically immortal. His continued existence after death depends upon God's gracious concern and power to keep him in existence for a fellowship with Himself and his fellowmen.

(*c*) The moment of physical death is not the moment of final judgement. There is, however, a final judgement at the end of history (Parousia). Final judgement here means a separation from God against which there is no further appeal. We must be agnostic in detail about the fate of particular individuals. We must, however, affirm the real responsibility of men, and therefore the genuine possibility of their final repudiation of God.

(*d*) Gehenna is the symbol for this final separation from God. It involves suffering by that very fact of separation. However, we have contended that such suffering is not 'endless' and that God will allow to pass out of existence those who finally (that is at the End) refuse to live in His world. That if this is the case, it would constitute a defeat for God, has to be admitted. Some people would argue that such a defeat is unthinkable on Christian assumptions. This, however, can only be maintained by denying the ultimate freedom of man to repudiate his Creator, and this we have refused to do. We may permit ourselves the larger hope that no man will be finally impenitent when history comes to an end. We cannot erect this into a dogma of the necessary salvation of all men. This latter hope may become fact. We cannot 'know' that it will inevitably be so. Nor should we, in presenting the gospel to men, play down the serious consequences of their decisions for personal existence after death and at the final summing-up of all things.

It remains to be said, however, that the Christian will be more concerned with heaven than with hell in the sense in which we have defined the latter. He will be more concerned to stress that God does not desire the separation of any man from the eternal love of the Father or from the redeemed community in which the rule of the gracious Father is accepted. He will need to emphasize that God's judgement of any man will be on the basis of a thorough knowledge of that man, his character and his true motives, a knowledge which by the nature of the case sinful and fallible mortals cannot possibly possess. At the same time, he must not shrink from continually reminding men, as he reminds himself, that it is man's divinely-given prerogative to shape his own destiny for good or ill, though God has gone to the uttermost limits of sacrificial love to lead him to a decision for abundant life rather than death.

Chapter Eight

Present Experience and Eschatological Hope

Our previous argument has been in favour of the real existence of persons after death. This was based upon the teaching of Jesus, the fact of His resurrection from the dead, and upon the strong case which can be made out on philosophical and even scientific grounds that mind is not reducible to physical process. The strongest basis of such a confidence in life after death remains for the Christian the character of God as holy love, and this in turn depends upon the conviction that in the life, death and resurrection of Jesus Christ, the true character of God has been disclosed to us. The real basis of the belief in personal immortality of an 'embodied' kind rests ultimately upon God, and not upon scientific evidence or philosophical reasoning. The Christian would do well if he is interested in apologetic to rest it fairly and squarely upon belief in God. This does not mean that certain men might not arrive at the conviction about life after death on scientific or philosophical grounds, or on religious grounds other than Christian ones. Plato and some forms of Hinduism stand as a permanent illustration of this, while spiritualists and those interested in psychical research still hope to show that belief in immortality is a part of a natural science which is more comprehensive and adequate than any achievement of scientific investigation up to the present. The Christian may keep an open mind on many of these issues, but in fact he is not greatly interested in any form of immortality without God. Since this has been the basic presupposition of our thinking on this subject, we have also deduced from the character of God the impossibility of endless punishment after death of a purely retributive kind. This no doubt will surprise many who have hitherto been perfectly certain that such a belief has the firm backing of Scripture. We have questioned this easy assumption and asked for a reconsideration of the evidence.

Now is the time to move a stage further and consider the notion of heaven as the goal and final bliss of the believer and of all who by their deeds of compassion have shown their love for the brethren of the Son of Man, even when they did not consciously know that in so acting, they were showing their loyalty to the Son of Man (Matt. 25: 40). It is not surprising that with the modern decline of confidence in God, the hope of heaven has likewise suffered an eclipse as the possibility of immortality in any form has become remote and improbable for many. However, we are not concerned to argue again about the adequacy of modern secular man's outlook upon life. Instead, taking our stand within the faith, an attempt will be made to sketch a consistent picture of heaven, given the basic soundness of the Christian view of God.

Heaven stands for the final self-fulfilment of man in God through the transforming power of His love mediated through Christ. If God is the active, creator God of Jewish and Christian faith, then heaven cannot be a static affair. In one sense, it is the end of a certain process of growth and development and transformation of the individual person. On the other hand, it is the beginning of a new existence if we reject the notion, as we do, that the believer perishes and passes out of existence at the very moment of fulfilment. Nor is heaven mere duration distinct from quality. It may very well involve duration and we have already questioned the total abandonment of all temporal categories when speaking of life after death. Yet it is not mere duration, merely going on and on in a temporal succession without rhyme or reason or without any relationship to God who transcends time. Heaven for the Christian is, after all, in Christ and this has personal as well as social implications.

We propose to tackle this question of heaven by a critical appraisal of a republished early work of Dr J. A. T. Robinson.[1] In view of many critical comments which will be made later, it should be said at the start that the purpose of this critique is not merely to show that the former Bishop of Woolwich is wrong. He deserves every credit for courageously dealing with the thorny field of eschatology when so many have left it alone or contented themselves with vague general statements. Dr Robinson not only deals with genuine problems of biblical exegesis, but with the questions which countless ordinary folk ask in this area of Christian belief. It is, however, our conviction that many of the things he says do not hang together in a consistent way. For this reason, in spite of his admirable intentions, the result of reading his book may be for many the weakening of the eternal

[1] J. A. T. Robinson, *In the End, God.*

hope, and doubt rather than certainty about life after death in a positive and worthwhile sense. His method of dealing with the eschatological issues opens the way to this danger, even though this is not what he intends. His habit of making a statement and then following it with its apparent contradictory opposite is in large measure responsible. We shall try to give examples in the discussion which follows.

Let us first of all indicate briefly the main points with which we are in full agreement, as will be evident from our previous statements, and which Dr Robinson rightly stresses as important and basic. What is said about the beginning and end of the present world-order, according to Robinson, must for the Christian depend upon insight into the nature and character of God mediated through history and in particular through Jesus Christ. The Genesis stories and the 'symbolic' pictures of the end are not literal scientific descriptions. On the basis of our present knowledge of God mediated through Jesus Christ, we extrapolate into the past and into the future. In this, of course, the Christian is not in principle doing anything different from the scientist when he, on the basis of present knowledge of the earth and of the universe, extrapolates into the past and the future and gives us his scientific 'myths' of the possible beginning and end of the present world process.[1] If it is argued that the scientist begins from present ascertained fact whereas the Christian begins from present wishful thinking, one can only say that this is based on the assumption that science necessarily involves a certain positivistic philosophy. This is not only not self-evident but it is not a universally shared conviction among all scientists. This said, however, we agree with Dr Robinson that eschatological statements about future states of affairs are deductions or extrapolations from a *present* experience of God, and in particular His love and concern for His children. If we ask how we arrive at this conviction, again we must as Christians say with Robinson 'It is love defined and vindicated for the Christian historically in the life, death and resurrection of Jesus Christ, in whom he (that is the Christian) sees all the fullness of God dwelling bodily.'[2] This is known in present experience. He then proceeds to draw certain conclusions from this starting-point. It means, among other things, that 'the Christian has no more knowledge of or interest in the final state of this planet than he has of its first'.[3] This again is true if it means that the Christian does not have to choose between

[1] A. Macintyre (ed.), *Metaphysical Beliefs.*

[2] Robinson, op. cit., p. 23.

[3] ibid., pp. 80-1.

Gamow, Hoyle or Bondi (the continuous creation and the 'big bang' theories), or that he is not in a position to describe in scientific terms what the state of this planet will be at the moment when organic life ceases. Whether this comes about through a change in climatic conditions, a new ice age, or the final burning out of the sun, or in the long term the running down of the universe to a dead level of heat according to the law of entropy, the fact remains that the Christian's present knowledge of God does not allow him to spell out in scientific terms the end of the process. The scientist may make a few reasonable guesses on the basis of his present knowledge, but this is another matter. However, the issue is far from settled. The Christian does have an interest in the destiny of all the persons who have lived between the beginning and the end. Furthermore, he cannot be neutral in the field of scientific theory if the theory in question is intended deliberately to exclude the God-hypothesis.[1] For example, it would be self-contradictory to assert my present knowledge of a loving God and then maintain that the world process originated in a 'big bang' which was the sheer accidental outcome of physical forces, even if these are etherealized into energies. In the same way, it would be inconsistent to hold the Christian view of God on the basis of present experience of His love and then assert that all who have died have perished for ever and that this same fate awaits the last generation when the earth becomes too cold for life in the manner of Bertrand Russell's apocalyptic description. The Christian could face with consistency and equanimity the end of all human life on this planet. He cannot with the same consistency face the total annihilation of the whole race of men. To this degree, he is interested in the final state of this planet inasmuch as the possibility of the end of all human life must raise in the acutest possible form the truth or otherwise of his present conviction that God is love.

It is clear that Dr Robinson is reacting strongly against the treatment of the eschatological symbols as a kind of pseudo-science, and rightly. This leads him to subordinate the past and the future to the present and to distrust a too naive use of temporal language in regard to the future. He prefers to talk of 'inaugurated' rather than 'realized' eschatology to express the truth that in the person and ministry of Jesus, the goal of history has already become present in history and the rule of God has begun. The word 'goal' here can only signify

---

[1] This phrase is loosely used in the manner that is frequent today. I do not intend to suggest that belief in God is for the Christian to be regarded as on the same level as the conjectural hypothesis of the scientist.

the meaning of history disclosed in the present and not a future event. 'That beyond which nothing can happen had already happened.'[1] This is a rather peculiar way of putting it. Obviously the world has not come to an end because Jesus has come. Nor in the ordinary sense can it be said that nothing could happen after Jesus because it is evident that many things have happened since His coming, whether we complain that all goes on apparently the same as before or whether we claim to discern with the eye of faith the golden thread of God's redeeming purpose in the Spirit-guided community of the Church. The confusion arises from the double use of 'goal' in terms of meaning and value and 'goal' as the end of a temporal progress. A Christian may believe that nothing could happen after Jesus which could either modify or improve upon the disclosure of God's holy love. The clue to the whole process of history, including the future, has been given in the present and in the personal action of God in Christ in history. With this we agree, for it is indeed an inevitable corollary of the Christian view of the Incarnation. This, however, cannot eliminate the seriousness with which time is taken in the chronological sense. Robinson, indeed, admits this, because he clearly acknowledges that God's purpose has not yet been fulfilled 'in the most final sense possible'.[2] The symbolic language of the Second Advent and the Last Day expresses this truth. If this is so, then some kind of future occurrence cannot be ruled out of court. The myth, he says, has to represent the triumph of God as a future event,[3] though it seems to be implied that it is not really an event. It is true that the idea of the End of history must be related to purpose, not merely to chronological futurity[4] but these are not necessarily antithetical. Why should not the fulfilment of a purpose involve chronological futurity, that is some time in the future? In effect, it must be so, as long as we are thinking of human history. And indeed, this is as true of the 'myths' of the beginning as of the end. Because Genesis is not literal science, it does not follow that the appearance of man as distinctly man was not an event in the past. It obviously was, however hazy we may be in our attempts to reconstruct or guess at the stages of the process which led to that event. The emergence of man is not a timeless truth but a historical event, even if we cannot give the precise date.

Why, then, should we not speak of the Parousia and the end of the age and of the final establishment of the kingdom as events? Certainly it would seem impossible to eliminate all sense of futurity

[1] Robinson, op. cit., p. 70.
[2] ibid., p. 70.　　　　[3] ibid., p. 78.　　　　[4] ibid., p. 33.

from the language we use about these things. They are not yet realities in the fullest sense possible, and from our human perspective they can only be in the future. One simple solution to all these perplexities would be to accept a thorough-going, Platonist, mystical interpretation of the biblical history and the eschatological language. Why not regard Jesus as the disclosure in time of the timeless truth of God's love? By a mystical relation to Him and to this truth, I could enter here and now into an eternal life which transcends time and space. Death then becomes simply a transition from the limitations of bodily existence and when it comes is of no great matter, provided I have the secret of eternal life now. History as successiveness in time now has only relative importance. The language of cosmic beginnings and ends could be abandoned completely, for we know nothing about them and even if we did, it would not be important. Even now I have eternal life: death will simply strip away for ever the dimness which inevitably belongs to life in the body. There is much in Robinson's writings which suggests that he is not without sympathy for this position. 'But it would be an equal misunderstanding to take the picture of the Last Things as historical prediction as it is to view Adam and Eve as personages of whom birth-certificates might theoretically be produced.'[1]

But this is ambiguous. Although we lack full knowledge of the emergence of man as man, there is no doubt that man did emerge. In fact, other things being equal, a birth-certificate could have been produced. The notion is not inherently nonsensical. Man did emerge at a point in the process which we can only describe as really 'in the past'. The fact that we cannot be more precise does not alter the fact that man did have a temporal beginning. By the same token, it is not absurd in itself to assert that history will have a temporal end.

But, Robinson might reply, the temporal end of the world is not what the Christian means by the Last Day. Granted, but the two things are not as disconnected as he thinks. If the Parousia and the Last Day stand, if only symbolically, for the taking up of the transformed historical process into the eternal life of God, then this can take place only when history has come to an end in time, and we have no other way of putting it except to say that it will be in the future. Indeed, Robinson has said earlier on that 'the ultimate truth about God is necessarily the final event in history'.[2] Does 'final' here mean final in terms of quality or final in the sense of a chronological end to the process of history or of the universe as such? To return to our

[1] Robinson, op. cit., p. 79.

[2] ibid., p. 48.

discussion of the Platonic-mystical alternative to a genuinely futurist eschatology, despite Robinson's apparent sympathy with such a solution, he rejects it. This is doubtless the result of the strong biblical influence which is also important in his thinking. He vigorously repudiates the attempt to turn the Christian gospel into a series of timeless truths. In view of his strong emphasis upon the present experience of eternal life in God, this seems rather surprising. No doubt he is thinking of timeless truths on the analogy of mathematics or the 'ideas' of Plato or highly refined philosophical or theological propositions. He wants to retain without any weakening the biblical idea of God's constant and purposive activity, embodied in the person of Jesus, and moving into the future towards a glorious fulfilment. To do this, he has to take 'time' seriously as involving significant movement and action from the past, through the present, and into the future. Nevertheless, if we can be certain of the truth and reality of God's love now through our present relationship to Jesus, why do we need a final event to confirm what we already know? He repeats the somewhat dubious antithesis between the Greek idea of timeless truth and the so-called Hebrew view that truth is what holds true at the end of time. If, however, we cannot be sure that love is the final truth about God until we see its triumph at the end of time, then how can we make deductions from our present experience of God with any confidence? Even though Jesus has lived, died and risen again, we do not yet see all things subject unto Him. The triumph of God's redeeming love is not yet unambiguously evident. We must, therefore, await the end of time until we can be absolutely certain of the ultimate victory, especially if truth is what holds good at the end of time, as he has previously asserted. We would have to conclude from this that the Christian lives in hope in the weakened sense of hope, since he cannot deduce with complete confidence from the present experience of God. Yet Robinson evidently wishes to do just this. He wants to justify the 'futurist' symbolism of eschatology as expressing the Christian's confidence, on the basis of present experience, that the future victory of the divine love and rule is not open to doubt.

It is doubtful whether he can do this convincingly unless he can provide a surer foundation in the present than he seems to be able to give to us. For example, he tells us that he is agnostic about what happens to himself after death.[1] Is he equally agnostic as to what happened to Jesus after His death? He is certainly so in regard to

[1] Robinson, op. cit., p. 23.

what happened to Jesus' body after His death.[1] His hope, he tells us, rests on nothing 'going on' or surviving dissolution.[2] It would seem that Robinson does not want to assert the preservation of the individual person after death, including Jesus. The traditional orthodoxy, which asserts the empty tomb and the aliveness of Jesus after death in the transformed body of the resurrection existence, can at least make a frank appeal to this stupendous act of God. On the basis of this 'miracle', he can then go on to deduce from his present experience of God's love and power, already vindicated in the resurrection of his Lord, confident anticipations as to the victory of this love at the end of history, notwithstanding all present experiences to the contrary.

But can Robinson really make this kind of appeal? In what sense has the Christian this confidence in the present that Jesus has really defeated death? Is Jesus really alive with God now or is He alive only in the hearts and minds of believers? There is obviously a great difference. If it be the latter, then we cannot be certain that Jesus survives death until we know whether we shall survive death, and this we do not know yet. The only alternative left is to say that in spite of our agnosticism about what happened to Jesus after death, we know enough about the love of the eternal God from His earthly ministry alone to be able to make confident affirmations about the ultimate victory of that love at the end of history. The 'myth' of the End, the Last Day, the Parousia thus becomes only a 'picture' designed to bring out the full implications of the present relationship.[3] In speaking of the Parousia, he remarks that the comparative ease with which the early Church survived the delay of the Parousia and the consequent disappointment only proves 'either that the hope of a Second Advent in any form was inessential to its preaching', or that the note of temporal immediacy was a 'misunderstanding of an urgency in itself independent of it'.[4] If this is so, then all that is required is that we become aware here and now of God's claim upon us, make our response to that claim in repentance and faith and enter at once into that eternal life which death cannot touch. The eschatological symbols then become only symbols of our present links with the eternal God and their futurist reference becomes of very limited importance indeed. But this is a thorough-going Platonizing of the eschatology, in which case it would be more logical for Robinson to abandon the Hebrew view of the significance of time and history and all its casting of hopes

[1] Robinson, op. cit., p. 24.
[2] ibid., p. 24.
[3] ibid., p. 75.
[4] ibid., p. 62.

into the future and concentrate upon the present 'mystical' experience of eternal life. Our feeling is that Dr Robinson has not resolved this tension in his thought and that he as a result finds himself in difficulties and inconsistencies.

Our conclusion then is that if the Christian hope is to be well founded, we must be able at least to assert the following things. God is love, for the past, the present and the future. This is shown in the personal activity of God in Christ and is vindicated against all the ambiguities of history by the fact that God raised Him from the dead and exalted Him to eternal fellowship and union with Himself in his glorified humanity. Jesus Christ, Son of Man and Son of God, is now alive after death. At the end of history (and this for us must mean the chronological future), Christ will manifest Himself again to the whole human family, past, present and future. He will make His presence (Parousia) known to the total fellowship of believers as transformed in Christ. Christians as persons will with Christ be taken up into the abiding and eternal fellowship of the Father. This will be a real event, though not necessarily a historical event in the normal sense of this word. It will be an event in that the Parousia brings to and end the long process of historical development. It will not be a historical event in the sense that the Parousia will inaugurate another historical epoch within the limits of this present space-time process. We, therefore, reject an earthly millennium and retain the concept of an eternal kingdom beyond space and time, as we at present experience and understand these concepts. It is not enough, therefore, to say that the Parousia only expresses symbolically the implications of our present experience of God. It does this and more. It points to a real consummation of the historical process and the taking up of all persons in Christ into the fullness of the divine life, when this age comes to a close. For this reason, we have to speak of it as future in more than a symbolical sense. This consummation is not yet.

This means that such words as 'literal' must be used with extreme caution. The Parousia is not literal in the sense that a new historical utopia on earth will be established which modern historians and scientists can examine with the methods they have devised for the exploration of this present world. It is literal in the sense that the union of Christ with His people at the end of history will be a meeting between a real Christ and a real community of persons. The fact that our embodied existence after death and the end of history will be different from our present bodily existence does not mean that we are not full persons. Thus, it is not enough to say that the Parousia and the ultimate kingdom are only symbols of a reality experienced in the present. They point to a real consummation and a genuine future existence still to be realized. Beyond this, neither faith, common sense nor reasonable conjecture can go.

However, in view of the recent concern with language and of temporal language in regard to the End, something more must still be said, even at the risk of tedium and some repetition.[1] It is not enough to say that truth's ultimate vindication is in a historical event, unless we give to that phrase a far deeper meaning than is customary. In discussing the contribution of the apocalyptic writers, in spite of their excesses and the tendency of some of them to try to construct chronological timetables, Robinson admits that they were compelled by the pressure of events to look for the justification of God, the vindication of the love and righteousness of God in a supramundane rather than a purely earthly Kingdom.[2] He also gives them credit for preserving the Hebrew conviction that history is a teleological process moving to an end or goal in a divine realm which is beyond history as we know it. On this point, it would seem that the apocalyptists were more in the right than Robinson. The ultimate vindication of God must lie beyond history as we know it. There are passages in which Robinson seems to agree with this, but how then can he consistently remain completely agnostic about his destiny as a person after death? It is very doubtful whether Greek influence alone was responsible for this development in later Judaism. It is more probable that the Jews, or some of them, were simply following out the inherent logic of their faith. Because they retain this eschatological outlook as against some cyclic views of history, it does not follow that they believed that the vindication of God's purpose was historical. After all, what could this mean? It could be intelligibly maintained in one sense if one could argue that the End of history means a perfect and everlasting kingdom of love and righteousness on earth. But Robinson is not inclined to any form of millennialism, naive or more sophisticated. Furthermore, if God's love is to be vindicated at the End in this sense, then such an earthly kingdom would have to be everlasting. Here again, Robinson knows his science too well to want to put all his hopes in the eternity of this present world. Furthermore, what would he do with all the millions of men and women who will not be there to share in the

---

[1] The following may be cited as illustration: O. Quick, *Doctrines of the Creed*; I. T. Ramsey, *Freedom and Immortality*; J. Pieper, *Hope and History*, not to mention many others, including Tillich of which we have already spoken.

[2] Robinson, op. cit., p. 50.

vindication of God in this historical event at the end? Will he bring them to life again in a miraculous resurrection? There is no hint that he will accept this possibility since he has already told us that he is quite agnostic about his 'going on' after death and the dissolution of the body. Austin Farrer has rightly pointed out that such concepts as society and history are in fact abstractions. The reality of history is the reality of persons and therefore, any vindication of God's love either now or in the future is inextricably bound up with the future destiny of individual persons, not the future of history in a vague abstract sense.[1]

Robinson asks in view of all the difficulties, 'would it be wiser to concentrate on personal immortality in a noneschatological context?'[2] The answer to this is that certainly we must concentrate upon personal immortality in some sense if we want to establish a meaningful understanding for the vindication of God's love in relation to persons and their destiny. If neither Jesus nor we survive death, then there is no final and satisfactory vindication of God. We do not need to repeat all the criticisms which we have made earlier of a radical this-worldliness as far as this issue is concerned. If, on the other hand, we are going to keep the eschatological context, then what does it preserve which a simple affirmation of personal immortality leaves out of account? We have already argued that the concept of personal immortality does not necessarily exclude a 'body' of some kind, provided this is not taken to mean the resuscitation and permanence of the present physical body.

The eschatological context preserves the notion of history, particularly as it relates to man's future on earth, as being a meaningful sphere of human activity within the context of the divine purpose. The very fact that it points beyond history enables it to treat present history in a positive way. We are not on this earth merely to prepare for a life after death, but to do the will of our Father who is in heaven. Such a positive conception can, of course, be combined with the hope of immortality without any contradiction. Indeed, both ideas require each other. The Christian does not have to choose between personal immortality and a hope for men's future in this world. He can still maintain that man cannot set a *priori* limits to what the grace of God operating through human freedom, might achieve in this world. On the other hand, he can still quite properly maintain that even if the perfect reign of God ever comes on earth, the ultimate vindication of

---

[1] A. Farrer, *A Celebration of Faith.*
[2] Robinson, op. cit., p. 53.

God's dealings with His people still demands an eternal realm, if His treatment of all those persons now dead and who will have died before the End is to be reconciled with His love. What is at stake here, as Canon Streeter maintained years ago, is not our sentimental and selfish desires but the character of God and the consistency of His action. Robinson rightly points out that 'for a purpose to be cut off at the very instant of achievement would not normally be regarded as fulfilled'.[1] This means that any future historical event, interpreted as a state of affairs on this planet or even in the galaxies, cannot by the nature of the case be the fulfilment of the divine purpose unless the earthly kingdom is everlasting and all the dead have a chance to share in it. Joseph Pieper has a striking passage which ends with these words: 'How can there be any talk of hope when the thing hoped for is so conceived that the being who is alone capable of hoping, namely the individual person, cannot have it?'[2] This means that the vindication of God cannot be in history, as history is normally understood as a sequence of events determined by the actions of persons in time. The fulfilment must be, if it exists at all for individual persons, beyond time as we know it, and beyond history, as we know it. The qualifying clause 'as we know it', is added because it is not a necessary corollary of our position that time can have no meaning for persons after death, or when this historical process has come to an end. What it does mean, however, is that the Christian hope cannot be vindicated by accepting the premises which determine the thinking of agnostics, humanists, socialists, Marxists and others for whom this world is the only world there is. To throw all hope into a future earthly state is in fact to destroy hope. No doubt howls of anger will go up at this reactionary statement, and the familiar gibe about 'pie in the sky' will be forthcoming. The fact remains that humanists of whatever variety have in fact dispossessed millions of human beings of their fulfilment since there is no place for the dead in their scheme of things, and even the present generation may not live to see their utopia.

[1] Robinson, op. cit,. p. 55.
[2] J .Pieper, *Hope and History*, p. 71.

Chapter Nine

Between the Times

Our discussion so far has been prompted by the extraordinary situation, aptly summed up by Joseph Pieper: 'A far more serious objection is that in all these anticipations of the future-whether grown in the soil of the idealistic philosophy of progress, of evolutionism, or the socialistic religious-there is scarcely any mention of death.'[1] In contrast, we have defended the New Testament belief that the vindication of the holy love of God and the fulfilment of man's deepest hopes demands a supra-mundane fulfilment beyond death. This has been expressed in the Christian tradition by such symbols and images as the Parousia, the End, The final judgement, heaven. We have also contended that the 'futurist' language is inevitable when we wish to speak of the End. The fact that our language must be symbolic does not mean, however, that it does not point to future 'realities'. The question still remains for future discussion as to whether modern man can live within this eschatological context with integrity, that is without denying the world-view which modern science and culture have produced. Does it still make sense to say that we live 'between the times', that is between the coming of Christ and the ultimate fulfilment of the divine purpose through His final manifestation at the end of history. If we cannot, then we cannot, though it has already been made clear what the alternatives are. We are left with a humanism which has no message of hope for countless millions of people. The Christian does not reject this latter alternative merely because he does not like it. He rejects it primarily because he believes that God has made Himself known in such a way that we are justified in looking to a future, not only in this world, but beyond death and the end of history as we know it.

Of course, it is a fact that millions of people never consciously think about death until it is forced upon them. Recently I was taken by a friend to the London Planetarium in which one sits below the dome of heaven and gazes at the awe-inspiring myriads of stars and

[1] J. Pieper, *Hope and History*, p. 69.

galazies. The commentator takes spectators on a guided tour of the most important of them. The sun suddenly begins to burn out and is reduced to a dull glow in the sky. We shiver, metaphorically, at the approaching cold and our own imminent end. On the surface, the spectators did not seem to be unduly alarmed. At any rate, one overheard, it will not happen for a long time yet. But we do not have to wait for the final challenge of the sun's extinction, but only for the passage of our three score years and ten. It is doubtful whether many people over middle age escape entirely some reflection upon their approaching end. It is then put aside and we try to believe that somehow things will be better on earth in the future if we put our minds to it. Instead of 'pie in the sky', we substitute pie in the earthly future— 'Ubi Lenin, ibi Jerusalem': But 'they are the emptiest of promises, are a totally abstract, deceptive consolation, offering man something that lives entirely beyond the here and now of his real existence.'[1]

The refusal to face these facts of our human mortality springs no doubt from a variety of causes. For some, it is simply morbid, that is, they do not want to think about it. For others, it is a distraction from building the earthly utopia. For others, it springs from a deeply rooted fear that if they faced the facts, the question of life's meaning would emerge with painful urgency and their own present spiritual emptiness would stand revealed. For some Christians, especially today, it comes from their reaction against a crude adventism or apocalypticism which is so concerned with looking for the signs of the end of history that they have no interest, time or energy for improving the present quality of human existence. Dr Robinson has told us that there is something absurd in asking modern men to spend their time scanning the horizon for the signs of the final cosmic catastrophe. Certainly one cannot read such a book as Norman Cohn's *The Pursuit of the Millennium* without feeling a good deal of sympathy for this reaction.

Nevertheless, we have good grounds for contending that such preoccupation with dates is not a true rendering of the New Testament faith. The danger is, however, that in repudiating all attempts to fix the date of the Parousia or coming of Christ, we are tempted to abandon all talk about a future consummation. This is equally a betrayal of the spirit of the New Testament. Oscar Cullmann has persuasively argued that 'It connotes a wrong approach to the problem of the hope of the New Testament to reduce it to the question: what is the date of the return of Jesus Christ.'[2] The following points emerge from his discussion of this theme:

[1] J. Pieper, *Hope and History*, p. 74.   [2] O. Cullmann, *The Early Church*, pp. 141 ff.

(*a*) Christian faith and hope take their rise from the decisive event which has already taken place, namely the life, death and resurrection of Jesus Christ, the sending of the Spirit, the present experience of the koinonia of the Spirit in the fellowship of the Church.

(*b*) On the other hand, the faith of the early Church did look forward. 'It is vital to maintain the temporal character of the eschatology.'[1] Even if we accept the validity of James Barr's contention that Cullmann has tried to deduce a too consistent and complete concept of time from the biblical material by a rather questionable lexicographical method, it is difficult to read the New Testament without coming away with the conviction that its writers were by their faith oriented to the future in a temporal sense.[2] The judgement of H. R. Mackintosh in the early part of this century still stands: 'It is no primitive fanaticism, it is part of the believing hope towards God, to expect a real close of history, a worthy denouement of the story of a world in which God has redeemed his people.[3]

(*c*) Both Jesus and the early Church did anticipate the end of history in the relatively new future. While it is true that no one reckoned on centuries of time elapsing between the resurrection and the return of the Master, that a period of time was envisaged before the End seems hardly open to doubt. Coupled with this is the firm statement of Jesus that He did not know the hour of the final consummation. This firm refusal to be concerned with precise dates must be given the fullest possible weight.

(*d*) In Jesus' thought, the temporal tension between the present age and the age to come is already abolished. The kingdom has already come near in Him and His community and continues henceforth to develop and unfold in time. 'The essential element in the nearness of the kingdom is therefore not the final date but the certainty that the expiatory work of Christ on the Cross constitutes the decisive stage in the coming of the Kingom of God.'[4]

(*e*) The presence of the Holy Spirit is the present guarantee that we live in the last stage of history which moves to the triumph of the divine purpose in the future.

(*f*) The End will come in God's own time when the gospel has been preached to all men. This fulfilment will be the creation of a new heaven and a new earth. 'This is why Christ will return to earth. The

---

[1] O. Cullmann, *The Early Church*, p. 144.

[2] J. Barr, *Biblical Words for Time*.

[3] H. R. Mackintosh, *Immortality and the Future*, p. 140.

[4] Cullmann, op. cit., p. 154.

decisive event will take place on earth because matter itself has to be recreated.'[1]

This is the framework according to Cullmann in which the gospel is set. We believe it to be substantially accurate, whatever reservations we may have about some of the details. The first question to be asked is whether such a framework is believable, tenable and even intelligible to modern man. Or is it, as Schweitzer said in his famous *Quest*, as dead as the moon? This question can be answered in a variety of ways. It can be argued that it is by and large unintelligible to modern man. Therefore, so much the worse for the New Testament. On the other hand, we might try to show that the reason why it is unintelligible and unbelievable to modern man is that the latter has a spiritual blind spot which prevents him from seeing what God has already done and therefore what God may be expected to do in the future. As we have already maintained, no eschatology is possible in a significantly religious sense apart from a doctrine of God which is its indispensable basis.

Before we deal with this question of intelligibility, however, there are certain problems which still call for consideration. If, as we have contended, personal immortality in an 'embodied' form and the Parousia as the future consummation of history are accepted as the plain implications of the New Testament faith in God, then what shall we say of the fate of the individual immediately after death? Certainly most people, if they are concerned with the subject at all, are more involved in their immediate destiny after death. From a Christian point of view, two basic factors must be taken into account. First is the Christian's personal assurance that he will not be separated from Christ at the moment of death. Secondly, since salvation is life in a new community, my personal fulfilment in Christ cannot be divorced from my participation in the final fellowship of believers including past, present and future generations. Since the redeemed community in this latter sense cannot obviously be complete until the end of history, salvation in the fullest possible sense must remain incomplete until God's purpose for the whole human race has been completed. It is not sentimentality for the Christian to ask—how can heaven be heaven without those I love? True Christian existence on earth, as after death, could be full and rich because it is 'in Christ'. Yet just as Jesus Himself is in one sense incomplete without the people He came to redeem, so we are incomplete until the love of our neighbour which Christ has inspired in us finds its fruition in the new com-

[1] Cullmann, op. cit., p. 147.

munity. The logic of Christian love requires that this be so, not only for the near and dear of our own families and our intimate friends, but for the whole race of men for whom Christ died.

What, then, of the individual at the moment of death? It has already been noted that Dr Robinson vigorously attacks an excessive emphasis upon the moment of death as both untrue to the New Testament and as involving an inadequate view of God. 'To be content with the individual eschatology of later Western Catholicism is to betray a sub-Christian view of the Fatherhood of God.'[1] The reason for this severe criticism lies in the fact that to make the moment of death the time of final judgement appears unjust. Few men and women, if any, are in such a spiritual condition at death as to merit either heaven or hell in the traditional sense. The division is not between black and white, the clear-cut separation of good and bad. Most of us at death are simply not yet fit for the rarefied air of the heavenly Himalayas.[2] Furthermore, the moment of death seems arbitrary. Some have a long life in which to come to repentance and faith. Others are cut off in their prime, not to mention those who die in infancy. Could a loving God assign some of His children to eternal bliss and others to eternal separation from Himself on the basis of what seems to be an arbitrary moment of time, namely physical death? We believe that the point is well taken.

The objections, however, are well known. It is argued that if men and women know that there may be a further chance of repentance and faith after death, then this will induce in them an attitude of carelessness in this present life. The sense of urgency in regard to basic moral and spiritual decisions will be undermined. We shall be more inclined to coast along with good intentions which are never brought to decision. Instead of believing that 'now is the day of salvation', we shall be inclined to say, 'Save me, O Lord, but not yet,' to adapt a famous word of Augustine used in another connection.

The first comment to be made is that our line of argument depends upon the acceptance of the Christian view of God and His purpose for men, with the consequent importance of our moral and spiritual decisions for time and eternity. Modern 'secular' man will hardly be likely to be impressed, since there is no God and this is the only world there is. Death is the final end and nothing can be done to change anything after death. We are what we are at death and nothing can change that. In any case, we shall not be alive after death to know

[1] J. A. T. Robinson, *In the end, God*, p. 44.
[2] H. W. Robinson, *Redemption and Revelation*, p. 308.

either blessedness of judgement. The questions we have raised, there-fore, only have meaning within the context of Christian faith and hope for the future. This does not mean that we have nothing to say to the secular man, but it does mean that we cannot speak meaningfully about eschatology until he has been brought to a significant experience of the reality and presence of God.

To argue that the removal of the moment of death for final judge-ment[1] leads to spiritual carelessness could only be true for the 'spec-tator', for one who stands outside the faith. Our argument is a deduc-tion from the character of the holy love of God, not from general philosophical considerations. No one who has met God in this sense could possibly become spiritually flippant because God in His com-passion has decided to leave the definitive act of final judgement until the Parousia. A similar issue arises when it is said that because we are under grace and not under legal codes, we are therefore free to do what we like or to indulge our unredeemed desires with impunity and a clear conscience. Paul long ago dealt with this question. We live under grace because of the costly, expiatory death of Christ in our behalf. How, then, can we go on sinning with a clear conscience? Nevertheless, it is important that Christians should consider these matters, because they are important for the way we regard our own spiritual calling and destiny and this in turn will determine the way in which we seek to present the Christian gospel to others.

We shall, therefore, turn now to consider the way in which some Christian thinkers have attempted to deal with this question. There are signs that after his long eclipse, Schleiermacher is once again claiming the attention of contemporary theologians. This is very under-standable, since he had a knack of penetrating the complexities of the theological tradition and making crystal clear what are the basic issues that are at stake. This does not compel us to accept his answers, but there is real value in seeing how he formulated the questions. When full account is taken of all the work of biblical investigation, criticism and exegesis which has been done since his day, it is doubtful whether any change has taken place in regard to the basic issues which he formulated. He is fully aware of all the difficulties involved in forming 'the idea of a finite spiritual life apart from that of a bodily organism'.[2] Since we have already considered this at some length, we shall be content here simply to note that Schleiermacher is fully

[1] E. Rosenstock-Huessy, *The Christian Future*.

[2] F. Schleiermacher, *The Christian Faith* (tr. H. R. Mackintosh and J. S. Stewart), p. 709.

aware of all the problems which are still being considered today in this connection.

Let us now turn to the issues which are raised if we refuse to make the moment of physical death the occasion of God's final judgement. If we put the final judgement at the end of history and associate this with a general resurrection and a judgement in the future, coincident with the Parousia, then certain questions immediately arise. One advantage of putting the final judgement at the Parousia means that we are not compelled to give supreme importance to the moment of the physical death to which Dr Robinson so strongly objects. This does not necessarily mean that men do not experience the judgements of God in the course of history. It does mean, however, that the final judgement, that is the irrevocable acceptance or rejection of men by God, only takes place at the End. This could be interpreted to mean that until the Parousia, no man's eternal future is finally and irrevocably settled. This again logically means that before the End, all men will still have their chance to respond to God in Christ. This would be true for all the pre-Christian generations of men, for non-Christians in the Christian era and those who have heard the gospel and for whatever reason have rejected it, and even for backsliding Christians who were converted but did not persist in the faith. The objection to this, which has already been noticed, would be that, since the time of the End is not known and for most men seems a long way off anyhow, the result would be to diminish the urgency and importance of a present decision for or against the gospel.

Assuming for the moment, however, that the final judgement is not made until the Parousia, what, then, is the condition of man at the moment of death? It would appear to be the logical corollary of the above that there must be some kind of intermediate state, that is a state of existence after death which continues until the Parousia. It is important at this stage of the argument to free ourselves from the doctrine of purgatory as developed in the Middle Ages. It will still have to be considered whether there is any truth at all in this historic doctrine. Suffice it now to insist that it is possible to envisage an intermediate state between the death of the individual and the Parousia which would not be identical with the doctrine of purgatory. The latter is based on the assumption that the decision as to heaven or hell is made at the moment of physical death. Purgatory is reserved for those who can be certain of getting to heaven in the End after they have been purified through suffering and helped by the masses of the Church sponsored by their friends. Whether one gets into purgatory or not is decided, however, at the moment of death. In other words, this Catholic eschatology is still based on the assumption that final judgement, positive or negative, concides with the moment of death.

The view of the intermediate state which we are putting forward implies that the final decision by God has not yet been taken. It still remains in the future, which is still genuinely open as far as ultimate salvation or rejection is concerned. This, we hold, is valid as a matter of principle. We have to be agnostic on matters of detail. For example, whether any men die so corrupted and deformed by evil that even at the end of this life, the possibility of change is non-existent, is something which we simply do not *know*. It may be so, but we cannot anticipate God's final judgement by drawing up a named list of those who would be in this category. We may feel with Dante that we have good grounds for putting some people in hell on the basis of their earthly performance alone. It is not difficult to think of some recent and contemporary figures whom we would very much like to assign to this category. But we cannot 'know' this in any detail or with certainty. All that we can say is that total and final repudiation of the divine offer must result in eternal separation from God. For the rest, Vengeance is mine, saith the Lord, and the End is not yet.

What, then, will be the state of Christian believers at the moment of death? We shall leave on one side for now the difficult question as to what constitutes a Christian believer. Not one who only gives formal assent to certain ideas about God and Christ and proceeds to live as if there were no God. Nor can we define a believer simply in terms of membership rolls of institutional churches. At the very least, however, a believer would have to defined in terms of repentance, faith, loyalty to Christ, and some evidence of the fruits of the Spirit. Here again, however, only God knows with the certainty of full knowledge of the heart who is a true believer in this sense. Assuming, however, that it is possible for some to say with sincerity and truth— I know in whom I have believed—our basic question remains. What is their state at the moment of death? They must have the assurance that death cannot separate them from the love of God in Christ. As Schleiermacher puts it: 'If the intermediate state be conceived as a conscious state, Christian faith certainly will insist that it cannot be a state devoid of fellowship with Christ.' If this were so, it would be equivalent to a lapse from grace[1] and even be a kind of punishment, the punishment of being deprived of God's presence and love. This is

[1] F. Schleiermacher, *The Christian Faith* (tr. H. R. Mackintosh and J. S. Stewart), p. 711.

unthinkable for the Christian believer who has died in the faith of Christ.

On the other hand, the intermediate state could be conceived as not conscious, that is a kind of sleep. As is well known, this represents an important strand in some Christian thinking over the centuries. It has recently been taken up again and accepted by Oscar Cullmann in a controversial little book.[1] On this view. the Christian will sleep until the Parousia when he will awake to the full consciousness of a blessed existence in Christ. Presumably the non-Christian will awake to some kind of conscious existence too. If he has never had a fair chance to accept the divine offer of salvation in this life, he will have it then. It must be admitted that the New Testament is by no means clear or unambiguous on this question as to whether the unbeliever will be raised again at the End. If during his earthly existence, the unbeliever has really rejected the divine offer and is sunk in evil, he will also be confronted with the same choice, but this will be determined by the sort of person he has become during this life. If as a consequence of his earthly actions his moral and spiritual deterioration has reached a point which precludes any kind of positive spiritual response, then God will have no choice but to reject him and permit him to pass out of existence. Since we have already rejected the idea of endless retributive punishment, annihilation of the wicked would seem to be the only alternative. Let it be repeated again, however, that according to our thesis, annihilation, if it takes place at all, or after a period of sleep or conscious existence in the intermediate state, will come, not at the moment of physical death but at the Parousia. The only other alternative is to say that once a man is confronted with the divine love in all its purity and holiness, free from all the misunderstandings and ambiguities of earthly life, he will gladly repent and yield himself to it. God will now fulfil His purpose in the Parousia of Christ until all men have so yielded. On this view, Nels Ferré would be right in asserting that there are no permanent problem children in God's universe. This gives us a doctrine of universal salvation in the manner of an Origen in the second century or a John Hick, a Nels Ferré or a J. A. T. Robinson in the twentieth century. The issue raised here centres upon the problem of the reality of human freedom to reject the divine love and the power of the divine love to overcome the most stubborn human heart. The Christian must certainly hope and desire such a consummation, though some Christians often speak as if heaven would be very unsatisfactory if

[1] O. Cullmann, *Resurrection of the Body or Immortality of the Soul?*

everyone were to get there, even if changed and transformed. Some ideas of heaven have been all too human, and we have tended to think of it as a kind of exclusive club which is only worth joining if some others can be excluded. Nevertheless, the more seriously freedom is taken, the more difficult it is to frame a dogma of universalism in which the salvation of all men is treated as rigorously necessary.

Other questions, however, must now be asked. Does the New Testament give us any firm ground for settling this issue as to whether the state of men after death and before the Parousia is conscious or a kind of 'sleep'? If we say, it will be conscious, then how is our existence in the intermediate state related to the 'resurrection body'? Will all men, good and bad alike, have such a body immediately at death which they will retain until the Parousia? In this case, as Schleiermacher says, it hardly seems necessary to have a general resurrection at the End because most men will have received their resurrection bodies. It is worth observing that for many Christians today, their thought is more Platonic than biblical. They think of the body decaying and the soul returning to God its maker. Why, then, trouble, about the End of history? The answer to this is that it betrays a purely individualistic and therefore, sub-Christian view of heaven and salvation. The idea of the End at least preserves the important idea that we cannot be saved in the full Christian sense apart from those who have gone before us and those who will come after. As a Christian, I am not concerned with my solitary flight to heaven, but with my incorporation in the total fellowship of Christ's redeemed people. If on the other hand, we say that our existence in the intermediate state will not be conscious, then the concept of a general resurrection at the End becomes a necessity since perpetual sleep could hardly be considered full and meaningful salvation for the Christian, whatever the Hindu vedantist may have to say about dreamless sleep. It also becomes necessary to ensure that the 'sleeping' Christian will one day know his acceptance by God in full personal consciousness. It may also be required to give meaning to the unbeliever's rejection by God, unless we believe that this has been confirmed at the moment of death, a view we have been inclined to question.

Are there any principles in our previous discussion which can help us to comment profitably upon these issues? It is obvious that the above ideas will irritate a certain kind of empiricist almost beyond endurance. This is what happens, he will say, when the Christian imagination is allowed to run riot, unchecked by any criteria for empirical verification. The fact remains that the questions are real and important ones for the Christian, and indeed for anyone who is not a thorough-going naturalist who sees death as the final end. Let us repeat again that we are not attempting to give a detailed literal description of what will happen at the End. It is obviously impossible to do this about an event which has not yet taken place. We are, however, attempting to lay bare the basic principles as to how God deals with persons, whether now, or immediately after death, or when history comes to a close. What is urgently needed is a clear account of the divine attitude which is consistent with His character as holy love as revealed in Christ. What is most important is that in our thinking about the end things, there should be no deviation from the character of God as defined by the Incarnation.

To take up again the questions we have just raised, it is our view that the New Testament supplies us with very little evidence one way or another as to whether the intermediate state is conscious or not. If it is unconscious (sleep), then obviously whatever is meant by the resurrection of the body will take place at the Parousia, and not before. If, on the other hand, it is a conscious awareness both of self and of Christ's presence through the indwelling Spirit, then such an existence must be a rich and full one. It cannot be simply an arid, shade-like existence reminiscent of the Hebrew Sheol or the Greek Hades. However, it would seem again to follow logically that if the believer is with Christ in this sense immediately after death, then so must the unbeliever be conscious. What, then, will his state be? The New Testament does not give us any help in answering this question, nor is there any suggestion that the believer after death will be with Christ while the unbeliever is unconscious (sleep). All that we can say, on the analogy of present experience, is that the unbeliever will be in a state of spiritual groping and uncertainty and deprived of the joy which he would have if he were in Christ. Nor can we assume, if we are consistent with the Christian view of God, that the grace of God will cease to operate in the intermediate state. There, as here, the unbeliever will exist in an environment which is willed by God. He is not, as in Sheol, cut off completely from the living God. He may be blind to the divine presence there, as he was here, but not because God is not there. Whether the experience of death will make him more able to know the divine love and presence and respond, we cannot say in any dogmatic fashion. We hope that this will be so. We cannot claim to know what dying does for a person's awakening to spiritual awareness of his need and the repentance this should arouse. 'Yet it is difficult to see why the mere event of dying, which has nothing to do with the essential values of personality, should miraculously turn sinners into saints.'[1] We believe that this is truer than the claims made by Ladislaw Boros for death as 'the moment of truth' and of decisive transformation.[2]

It is clear from this discussion that we frankly admit to a considerable degree of agnosticism about the intermediate state. It is clear that Helmut Thielicke in his fine book *Death and Life* is equally cautious about making too many definite statements about the intermediate state. On the basis of specific New Testament references (Luke 16: 19 ff.; Luke 23: 43; 2 Cor. 5; Phil. 1: 23; Rev. 6: 9), he thinks that the most we can say must be in terms of Being-at-Home with Christ.[3] The basic thing to be said about the believer after death is that he has a Lord who will not desert him in death. With this we are in substantial agreement. The fact remains, however, that if we reject with Thielicke any splitting up of the 'I', the real person, into body and soul, then we are compelled to affirm the reality of that full personhood after death, even if we leave the precise nature of that 'embodied' existence unspecified in detail as the New Testament does. If the Lord does not desert me at death, and if my destiny cannot be separated from the consummation of the divine purpose at the Parousia and the final judgement, then the reality of the whole man's communion with his Lord at death and at the end of history must be affirmed. At least this minimum must be said about the intermediate state. We may not be able to spell out in detail what Thielicke calls the 'subjective structure of continuing existence' after death. We cannot describe in detail an existence which is not yet ours. Yet we must assert the reality of it as a full personal existence in communion with the Lord. Otherwise we leave the believer with a mental blank rather than a positive hope in his thinking about his destiny at death or at the End of history, or both. Thus, our agnosticism about the intermediate state cannot be total. If it were, we would be denying the ultimate goal and its achievement in Christ at the Parousia, and this we are not entitled to do. We can speak with confidence of the believer being with Christ after death. We can also say that, even for the believer after death, there is still a looking forward to the ultimate consummation. Beyond this, we must await with patience the making of all things plain.

[1] H. W. Robinson, *Redemption and Revelation*, p. 308.
[2] L. Boros, *The Moment of Truth*.
[3] H. Thielicke, *Death and Life*, p. 215.

What, then, of the resurrection body? Do all men receive it at the moment of death, believer and unbeliever alike or only believers? This very way of framing the question implies a body-soul dualism which we have already seen some reason to question on biblical grounds. We have already pleaded for personal immortality in an 'embodied' form while rejecting the notion of a literal resuscitation of our present flesh or physical body. A continuity of real personal existence is what is, therefore, at stake. Our position is neither Greek nor Hebrew in any simple sense. We are denying that personal continuity demands the same, identical physical body. On the other hand, we are rejecting a conception of existence after death of a purely disembodied kind. Some would say that this is impossible and that we must make a simple choice between the one or the other. This again we have denied as not required by the New Testament understanding of the matter. If our position is tenable, then there seems no reason why the Christian at the moment of death should not enter upon the new mode of existence of an embodied kind in Christ. He does not await the general resurrection at the end in order to be changed from a present ghost-like existence after death to become a real person again. The idea of being in Christ as only half a person does not make sense. Why, then, does the concept of a general resurrection need to be retained at all?

Our answer to this is along the following lines. The general resurrection does not stand for the transition from an incomplete personhood to becoming a real person in the full sense. It stands for the entry of the believer into full communion with the whole body of the faithful at the End when Christ claims his whole people. After much criticism of Dr Robinson, we are glad to acknowledge his contribution to this issue in his analysis of the meaning of 'body'. We believe that he has given valid insights on this issue. 'Body' in Hebrew and New Testament thought does not stand for that which separates men from each other but for that which unites them. It is the symbol for human solidarity and, therefore, for the final communion of persons. There is no fundamental inconsistency, therefore, in asserting real personal existence after death and retaining 'the general resurrection of the body' as a symbol for the fulfilment of the divine purpose in the corporate reality of the kingdom, the communion of saints and of just men made perfect. In the New Testament, this general resurrection is linked with the idea of the last judgement. In much theology in the past century and a half, where it has not been eliminated altogether, the last judgement has been seen as a purely judicial act of God with the emphasis upon his final rejection of the wicked. Too little has been said about the positive side of judgement as the bringing of all believers into full possession of that blessedness which none can experience as isolated individuals, but only as a 'body' of believers united in love.[1]

To sum up, we have attempted to defend the idea of the intermediate state between death and the Parousia and the end of history. We affirm this, not on the basis of any magical clairvoyance of the future but as a necessary implication of the character of God as holy love. If God is such, then death is too arbitrary a point at which a man's ultimate destiny can be decided. We must then have the courage of our convictions and admit that the intermediate period must allow for spiritual growth, for deeper repentance and faith, for a first acceptance of the gospel by those who have never heard it. But can we logically deny the opposite, namely the possibility of retrogression, of new sin and failure, even of a believer who has died in Christ, a falling away in the intermediate state into faithlessness and disobedience? In this case, no Christian could die with confidence because he could not be sure whether he would deny Christ in the intermediate state and thus forfeit the fellowship of God in Christ which was the comfort of his dying moments. On the other hand, if we freeze the spiritual state of believer and unbeliever at the moment of death and admit of no significant spiritual changes in the intermediate state, then why postulate the latter at all? We have returned full circle to the view of physical death as the moment of final judgement with all the difficulties which we have seen to attach to this idea.

There are only a limited number of ways around this problem. We can say that that the believer who dies in Christ cannot fall away, but only continue pressing on until he has attained to the fullness of the stature of Christ. This only leaves the possibility for the unbeliever of turning to God in faith or continuing on his path of decline and disobedience. In other words, the non-Christian has a chance to become Christian, but not the Christian to become non-Christian. But is this not quite arbitrary and a *reductio ad absurdum* of the whole argument? But what kind of assurance does the Christian have even now in this life that he will not in the future fall away? In the past, doctrines of election, predestination and irresistible grace have been developed to meet this need. The fact, however, remains that no assurance can be based on a relationship to God which destroys

[1] See the illuminating study by J. P. Martin, *The Last Judgment in Protestant Theology from Orthodoxy to Ritschl*.

those personal responses of repentance, faith, commitment, trust and love which are integral to a genuinely personal relationship. In pure logic, if there is such a thing, the Christian cannot be absolutely certain that he can never deny God, any more than he can be sure that he will never betray his wife or his friends. Assurance can only be the fruit of a lived and experienced relationship, not the conclusion of a logical argument, even if it is a theological one. Obviously, we must discard a Pelagian or atomistic conception of character. Patterns of stability are built up in character for good or evil based upon previous decisions and commitments. Even if he is not perfect, and no man is, he may have as a Christian the humble certainty that the transforming grace of God in Christ has made him such a man as cannot (that is morally and spiritually *cannot*) deny the God in whose love he is rooted and anchored. But it is a spiritual certainty, not a logical one. Our assurance springs basically, not from a subjective feeling of certainty, but from our trust in the Lord who can hold us up when we are in danger of falling.

We come back now to the earlier question raised in the last of Cullmann's points: how shall we conceive of the return of Christ at the End to bring the whole of history to its destined fulfilment in Him? Let us recall Cullmann's exact language: 'This is why Christ will return to earth. The decisive event will take place on earth because matter itself has to be recreated.' It is this kind of language which perhaps causes the greatest difficulty for many in our day. Why does Cullmann use this kind of language and what is at stake, if anything? The importance of taking 'futurist' language seriously has been emphasized in our previous discussion of the New Testament eschatology. On the other hand, millennialism has been repudiated because of its slender foundation in the New Testament and its complete absence from the teaching of Jesus. The Parousia has been accepted as a symbol which points to a genuine reality at the end of history, but why insist, with Cullmann, that this final event must take the form of a return to earth? The reason given by him is that 'matter' itself has to be recreated. This raises many large and difficult questions which we can only touch upon briefly here. Cullmann, I take it, is not saying that Jesus will return to establish a kingdom on earth under the same physical and biological conditions which obtain at present. On the other hand, he wishes to retain the idea of some kind of total transformation at the End of the world process which includes both nature and history. A not dissimilar idea is found in Teilhard de Chardin when he speaks of the cosmos unified in Christ and translated to a transcendent realm which will leave behind space and time in the form we experience them now and will, therefore, be beyond death. But what can Cullmann mean by saying that 'matter itself has to be recreated'? Given the Christian understanding of God as Creator and His relation to the created order, which includes what we call matter, there would appear to be nothing inherently inconceivable in the idea that God could transform the present order of things to produce a new environment for man in a new mode of existence strikingly different from the one we know now. The notion of the transformation of energy, if we think in these terms and not in those of 'billiard-ball' atomic physics, is an idea neither irrational nor at variance with modern science. If this possibility of a complete transformation of the present cosmos seems incredible to modern man, the reason is that he thinks of nature as not guided to any ultimate goal. This is understandable if nature, as so far explored, is regarded as exhausting the creative possibilities of genuinely new and novel situations and events. Even physics would hesitate to be dogmatic in this sense. If God is real in the Christian sense, then it is even less reasonable to close the door to future transformations of the cosmos beyond our present imagination or conceiving.

This raises the problem often discussed in the past by theologians concerning the eternity of the world. It is well known that Aquinas accepted the point that the beginning of the universe in time cannot be demonstrated by philosophical or scientific reasoning, even though we may feel justified in affirming it on the basis of scriptural authority. Presumably on the same grounds, we could affirm that the notion of an end of the present cosmos is hardly conceivable unless Scripture gives us grounds for so thinking. What, however, could the claim that the universe is eternal really amount to? Not the eternity of any fixed form of the cosmos, for if the process philosophers have taught us anything, it is that all is flux and becoming. What we call the universe has been changing for millions of years and is still in constant transformation. Admittedly our minds get into difficulties at the thought of an absolute end. As Canon Quick reminded us some years ago: 'The notion of something which happens strictly last in time is self-contradictory.'[1] Certainly if our previous defence of the reality of personal existence after death and therefore after the end of history is accepted, then the Parousia and the transformation of the present cosmos cannot be an absolute end, for this would mean that there would be nothing at all. On this supposition the Parousia is both an

[1] O. Quick, *Doctrines of the Creed*, p. 245.

end and a beginning of a new cosmos and fresh forms of personal and corporate existence. However, our minds are equally in difficulty with the idea of sheer endlessness when, as Quick says, we try to give it a concrete and not merely a mathematical significance. Quick suggests that we should rather work with the idea of end as 'completion of a process by bringing it to its purposed end'.[1] This is certainly helpful if we confine our thinking to the redemptive purpose of God for His human children which reaches its purposed end at the Parousia. But are there no other ends which God can pursue after the Parousia? We often assume that a teleology, that is a process directed by divine purpose in interaction with human freedom, depends upon the struggle against sin, guilt, weakness and death and that when these have been removed, the idea of purpose and goal loses all meaning. This, however, is by no means self-evident. Heaven, if we may use the traditional category for a moment, may permit of new ends and goals to be accomplished. If God is the Creator-God of biblical faith, and even perfected men and women are real persons and not static ciphers, then this would seem necessary unless we are going to empty the notion of heaven of any kind of significant activity. Origen in the second century contended for an endless and unceasing series of aeons, since God cannot exercise His sovereignty and providential care in a vacuum. He must have a created realm of some kind since He is a Creator by nature. In our view, this is not a heretical idea. The Christian need only oppose the eternity of the world if by this we mean that man's destiny is confined to this present cosmos and that death has the last word over man. This he must reject in the light of the gospel. If the eternity of the world means rather that God's creative activity never ceases and that even in heaven He still provides His creatures with worthwhile goals to puruse, then the idea is not for the Christian at least absurd.

No doubt some will be already reacting impatiently against this whole idea. These questions, it will be argued, only arise if one applies naive and anthropomorphic views of clock-time to an eternal realm where they no longer apply. Yet there is no such easy escape from the problem of time, the most mysterious and baffling of all philosophical and religious problems. Of course, as we have already seen, there are other available 'solutions'. The reality of time and change can be denied outright. Despite appearance, nothing ever changes, and underneath the flux there is one unchanging reality to which no human adjectives can apply—it is not this, not that (The Hindu *neti*

[1] O. Quick, *Doctrine of the Creed*, p. 246.

neti). This, however, reduces persons to ripples on the cosmic ocean. It cannot logically entertain the idea of a personal immortality. The problem of time is solved by the denial of the ultimate reality of persons, except in a fleeting and temporary sense. This solution is not open to the Christian. As long as the distinctness, reality and possible immortality of persons is allowed, then 'time' in some form remains to baffle us. We may accept Quick's dictum that 'real time is measured, not by clocks or calendars or astronomical statistics, but by the process of God's work'.[1] Obviously, if the present cosmos is radically transformed at the Parousia, we shall not carry watches in heaven. Our time-scale will not be measured in terms of the solar system, which will presumably have passed away in the form in which we now know it. Does this necessarily mean that the 'now' and the 'not yet', the awareness of duration, will have completely ceased? The Christian is not obliged to claim a preternatural knowledge of the next world in order to make his response to this question. The basic deduction which he must make from his present knowledge of God demands an affirmation of a continuously creative and not static God, the reality of persons here and now and God's loving purpose to bring them to the self-fulfilment in Christ and in the corporate body of His people, the reality of such persons and such community after death and the end of history under the care of a God who is still active and who will still have significant activities for His children to perform. There seems to be no way of preserving these basic truths without the courageous use of temporal categories both for the present universe and what comes after it ends with God's goal achieved. Admittedly, we cannot imagine the forms of space and time in the new heaven and the new earth. When matter has been recreated, in Cullmann's language, the new order of being will be radically different in many ways and we only see now in a glass darkly. Notwithstanding, it is less misleading to use the language of time, even for existence after the Parousia, than to allow the significance of personal reality and activity to be swallowed up in a static eternity or a featureless Absolute.

[1] O. Quick, *Doctrines of the Creed*, p. 249.

Chapter Ten

Philosophical Excursus on Time

The last two chapters have been devoted to a consideration of the ways in which we may think of the fulfilment of the divine purpose in relation to the destiny of the individual and of the human race as a whole, that is the sum total of all persons who have lived on this planet, past, present and to come. A major objection to what we have tried to do in these chapters might very well be that a naive and uncritical view of time has been assumed. This is only partially true, though it must be conceded that a view of time as flowing from the past through the present into the future has been assumed. Furthermore, temporal language has been frankly used of the mode of existence of persons after death and the end of history. This was found to be inevitable if certain truths were to receive reasonably adequate expression. In this chapter we shall turn aside for a brief look at some of the philosophical issues which arise in this connection. In dealing with these, it will be necessary to ask the question as to whether Christian language about personal immortality and eternal life can be just as well expressed when all temporal significance is eliminated. It is inevitable that we should start with the famous and oft-quoted comment of St Augustine in the *Confessions*, which may now be rather hackneyed but which still makes its point very forcefully. 'What, then, is time? If no one asks me, I know: if I wish to explain it to one who asketh, I know not.'[1]

Before, however, the strictly philosophical questions are asked, it will be worth while to ask whether there is such a thing as the biblical conception of time. It is well known that this has been a subject of keen debate in recent years and is indeed still so. What is meant by enquiring about the biblical conception of time? It is not being asked whether the ordinary Jew had an awareness of past, present and future like the rest of us. It is obvious that he had. Nor whether he had

[1] Augustine, *Confessions*, XI (XIV).

a calendar, because again it is clear that he had. Likewise he was quite well able to put things in chronological succession. What we are really asking is whether the Jew in biblical times ever tried to answer the philosophical question: What is time? and whether there is in the Bible any attempt to explain how time, as normally experienced, is related to God and to eternity, eternity here being defined as a quality of divine existence which is beyond change and successiveness as we know it. Professor James Barr has pointed out the almost complete absence from the Bible of such statements as:

> Time is the same thing as eternity.
> Paul teaches that eternity is not timelessness.
> Time is the field of God's action.
> Time is known by its content.
> God created Time.
> There is a Time, other than our time, which is God's Time.[1]

This fact should put us on our guard at once against expecting from the Bible a view of time and eternity consistently worked out and expressed in philosophical terms. The reaction to this, however, can be twofold. It could be said that the philosophical question is improper and impossible of being answered in the nature of the case. The difficulty with this 'solution' is that, despite the philosophical reticence of the Bible, our minds persist in putting certain questions to the biblical material. This has been evident in our own previous attempts to work out the implications of the eschatological perspective of the New Testament. One is forced to ask certain questions about the future destiny of the individual person and of the race after death. This is not a desire to gaze into a crystal ball and see in detail those things which have not yet taken place. Rather it comes from the desire to understand the full implications of what it means to say that God is love and to assert the ultimate victory of that love in relation to men and women who, on Christian assumptions at least, are His children.

Oscar Cullmann has insisted in *Christ and Time* and other writings that if we want to understand early Christianity, we must forget all philosophical attempts to understand time. We must see things from the early Christians' perspective, and that means to think of eternity as endless time flowing from the past through the present and into the future. The end of the present cosmos, therefore, does not mean

[1] J. Barr, *Biblical words for Time*, p. 132.

the end of time. It means the transition to a new order of existence in relation to God which, for the finite creature, will still be in some significant sense a temporal existence. Likewise, in his assumptions, Cullmann cannot logically speak of a beginning of time, such as the suggestion of some earlier Christian thinkers that the world and time were created together. Time is endless, whether we look to the past or the future. This, thinks Cullmann, is the biblical view. If as Christians, we accept the Bible as authoritative because it is the divinely-given vehicle for the transmission of the revelation, then we shall accept their view of time, asking no questions, that is no philosophical questions, which arise from a non-biblical perspective.

It is equally well known that James Barr has criticized Cullmann on two counts. The first concerns his lexicographical method. Cullmann is accused of concentrating upon the meaning of certain biblical words and deriving from them certain theological concepts which are then regarded as valid. The most notorious is the contrast between *chronos* (that is clock-time—time as measured succession) and *kairos* (filled time—time with a spiritual content when filled with the activity of God). Barr's point is that whatever merits there may be in this distinction of a general theological or even philosophical point of view, the distinction cannot be based on the actual usage of these words in either a classical or a biblical context. There is, contends Barr, no single, fixed usage of words. This changes from place to place, from one cultural and historical context to another. We must pass, therefore, from the study of words in a simple etymological sense to a study of the meanings which certain groups of words have in a particular context. There is nothing sacrosanct about either Greek or Hebrew words as such. Words, he insists, do not 'disclose something of the realities they express'.[1] The word 'dirt' reveals nothing about dirt as such nor does the word horse about horses. This applies equally at the lofty level of theological discussion. This means that if we want to know if there is a biblical view of time, we cannot appeal to a fixed, unchanging significance of kairos as filled time. We can only study the actual usage of men at a particular period and seek to penetrate to the nature of their 'thought', to try and discover what they were trying to say and express when they used words in a certain way. It is important to remember that Barr is not categorically denying that Cullmann may have a reasonable case for his view of time as endless and unilinear as far as New Testament thought is concerned. What he is contending is that such a theological conception

[1] J. Barr, *Biblical words for Time*, p. 134.

of time cannot be simply deduced from the study of words in the way adopted by Cullmann. If such a view of time is to be commended as the one most consonant with the biblical understanding of God and His relationship to history, so be it. This, however, will have to depend on general theological considerations, not upon the study of isolated biblical words conceived of as intrinsically possessing built-in theological concepts. Barr's own conclusion is that the Bible does not explicitly raise the strictly philosophical questions about time and eternity. If we wish to develop some reasonably consistent scheme of thought in regard to these issues, then this must be the work, not of biblical but of philosophical theology.

We believe that Barr's fundamental point is well taken and the rest of this chapter will, therefore, be an essay in philosophical theology. The question about time then takes on a somewhat different appearance. We still have to grapple with the fundamental issue. Does the philosophical analysis of time throw any light at all upon the way in which the Bible's use of temporal language can be understood? There is no disagreement about the fact that the Bible does use temporal language both about God and man. Yet it still has to be asked whether the philosophical analysis of time necessarily has purely negative results as far as the biblical usage is concerned. For example, are we now faced with a drastic reinterpretation of biblical temporal language in order to avoid the antinomies and intolerable paradoxes which emerge if we take such temporal language in a naive sense? But what is 'naive' in this connection? What criteria are being employed to justify the use of the word 'naive' at all? Is the use of temporal language in the Bible merely an accommodation to the weakness and limitations of human thought? Can we express the same basic truths by a complete exclusion of temporal language? Can the reality to which the Parousia points be indicated without a reference to the future? Can personal immortality be validly and meaningfully defended without any reference to an after-life? It is clear that we are embarked upon a difficult enterprise with far-reaching implications, not only for philosophical theology but for the practical expression of our faith in the actual living of the Christian life in hope.

There are three basic questions which can be asked about time:

(a) Is time real or unreal?
(b) Does it move in one direction only or is it reversible?
(c) Does it have a beginning or an end, or is it infinite, that is never ending?

It is obvious that for most people, the answer to (a) is self-evident. Of course, time is real because all our activity is measured in terms of it. Do we not live by the watch, especially in our highly integrated technological societies? Yet even the average man today, thanks to space shots, moon probes and satellite communication, is vaguely aware of the mystery of time. When he reflects, he knows that our calendar and our clocks are relative to the solar system of which our earth happens to be a member. We all know these days that if we lived on Jupiter, the calendar would be a very different affair. Nevertheless, for ordinary practical purposes, the present method of time reckoning works well enough.

When we move into the more sophisticated area of physics, the question takes on another form. To ask the physicist whether time is real is to ask him whether 'the changes—biological, astronomical or atomic by which we measure time, and which we measure by it, are real'.[1] Since the job of the scientist is precisely to measure change in this sense, he must perforce say yes to the question whether time is real. Whatever philosophical doubts he may have, in practice he must accept the reality of time in the sense required for his scientific calculations and predictions. Philosophers, however, have for various reasons questioned the reality of time. Not that they would deny the practical value of such scientific measurements of change. After all, even philosophers consult their watches and sometimes act by the clock, as did Immanuel Kant, who walked to the university so regularly every morning at the same time that the citizens were able to set their clocks by him! Nor do philosophers deny that we have a psychological experience of duration and that for practical purposes we have to live and speak in terms of past, present and future. When they talk, if and when they do, of the unreality of time, they appear to be saying that, whatever our present experience, reality is very different from its appearances. From our limited human perspective, time may seem to be a simple flow, but when we try to think about our experience, the paradoxes for our thinking which then arise become so formidable that the only option is to say that time is not ultimately real. The 'really real', if the odd expression may be permitted, cannot be in time nor can it change in the manner we think it does. F. H. Bradley argued in this way, contending that change cannot be thought of without contradiction. Earlier still, Kant had argued that if time had not beginning, eternity has already elapsed, which is inconceivable. The notion of time, without beginning or end, cannot be rationally

<hr>

[1] S. A. Goudsmit and R. Claiborne, *Time*, p. 165.

understood. In one sense Kant is saying that time is ultimately unreal because it is self-contradictory for thought. On the other hand, Kant makes time and space the two fundamental categories by which our minds shape the forms of all human experience. In this sense, time is real enough for most of us. It is only unreal if we are asking what reality is 'in itself' but this, says Kant, is not given to human reason to know.

It would appear as if human attitudes to time and change are in part determined by temperamental considerations. From Parmenides onwards, there always seem to have been some people who have a deep psychological longing for the unchanging, the fixed, the stable, the secure. In so far as time involves change, it is unattractive to them, even abhorrent. Their aim is to arrive by some means or other at a reality which is not subject to change and, therefore, presumably not subject to time as we know it. This desire for the permanent and the unchanging is probably to be found in all human beings with varying degrees of intensity. In some, it becomes so powerful that it determines their whole manner of thinking, even when it leads to the apparent absurdity of saying that time is unreal. This is characteristic of philosophers and mystics, and sometimes of philosophers who are also mystics or vice versa. The significant names in this connection are Parmenides, Plato, Plotinus, Spinoza, some form of Hegelian idealism, though perhaps not Hegel himself. Professor J. N. Findlay has recently contended that Hegel is misunderstood if thought of as a metaphysician of the transcendent. 'There can be no doubt at all that Hegel sees what is "absolute" in nothing which lies beyond the experiences and activities of men.'[1] We must leave the Hegel experts to debate this issue of the correct exegesis of the Master. There seems little doubt that some idealists, taking their inspiration from Hegel, have tended in a monistic direction which denies or belittles the reality of time and change in any ultimate sense. This philosophical tendency may or may not issue in a mystical approach. 'No indefinitely prolonged succession of events satisfies the non-progressist type of mind. It wishes rather to anchor itself to the heart of the real, "where is no variableness nor shadow of turning".'[2]

It does not need to be emphasized how in religion, and in Christianity in particular, this thirst for the Eternal as the unchanging has played and still plays a decisive part in the lives of many believers. Our hymns (for instance 'Abide with me') still afford eloquent witness

[1] J. N. Findlay, *Hegel*, p. 20.
[2] A. E. J. Rawlinson, *Essays on the Trinity and the Incarnation*, p. 342.

to this fact. The greater the emphasis upon the Eternal as the timeless and the unchanging, however, the greater become the problems which arise for a specifically Christian faith. Does an unchanging Eternal mean a 'static' Eternal? How is this combined with the biblical notion of a living and active God deeply involved in History and therefore in time and change? And if the divine involvement in history is real and not mere appearance, then must there not be a sense in which God is also in time and subject to change?

For the moment it is enough to point out that this issue has led some philosophers and a good many Christian thinkers to seek to rehabilitate the reality of time as against all such monistic tendencies to belittle it. A certain type of philosopher will ask: If time is only an appearance, how can we explain the fact of the appearance and the very vivid sense we have of its apparent reality? In our very secular, this-worldly, technological and activist Western culture, this conviction of the reality and importance of time and change is only emphasized the more. Add to this the theory of evolution and the philosophical view of the world process as a perpetual becoming, and we have a violent swing of the pendulum against any philosophy or religion which seeks the real in the unchanging Eternal. The popularity of the process philosophy in North America at the present time and its Christian adapters is an illustration of this tendency. If, however, reality is process, then we are faced with the other problem as to whether there is any permanence within the never-ending process of change. It was Bergson in his early work who popularized long before Whitehead that it is change that is real and the supposed identity of the changing thing that is illusory. He sums it up thus: 'there is nothing but change: there are no things that change.' Real time can only be lived (*la durée*—duration). It cannot be spatially conceptualized Logically enough, the early Bergson was not committed to a view of God in the classic Christian and theistic sense, for this was hardly compatible with his view of change. He was equally logical in rejecting teleology, understood as a goal towards which the whole process moves. Both God and teleology would in his view be destructive of the spontaneity and at the human level the freedom which characterizes all change, for it would mean that *tout est donné, rien de nouveau*. This brief comment on Bergson should not be taken as a adequate summary of his thought as a whole. The mature Bergson of *Les Deux Sources de la Morale et de la Religion* is obviously seeking to recover the other pole of the truth, namely the reality of the eternal as the permanent and the abiding.

Before we try to give a judgement as to whether or in what sense time is real or unreal, our other two questions must be considered.

(*b*) Does time move in one direction only or is it reversible? Common sense says it moves in one direction, for the simple reason that we are powerless to reverse the process of birth, growth, maturity, death and decay which constitute our life in the body. However much we may toy with the idea of time-machines and crossing the time barrier, so beloved of the writers of space-fiction and of certain TV programmes, in practice we are forced to see our lives moving into a future and ourselves as powerless to reverse the process. If we move beyond 'common sense' into science proper, we find the physicist on the side of the irreversibility of the time process. Although in theory the physical forces involved might just as well operate successfully in the reverse direction, in fact they do not, and the law of entropy strongly suggests that they will not. 'When we take a hard look at the basic laws governing physical change, we find that most of them seem to operate equally well in either direction.'[1] On the other hand, the law of entropy, based on the empirical fact that heat will flow only from a warmer body to a cooler body, never the reverse, leads to the view of the one-way nature of time. It, then, becomes an appropriate symbol to speak of the 'arrow of time'.[2] On the theological level, we have found Cullmann insisting on the unilinear and irreversible nature of the time process according to the biblical understanding of the matter. It might seem at first glance as if common sense, science and theology were all agreed on this all-important issue and such an agreement would indeed be remarkable and impressive! Unfortunately, there is a good deal more to be said. Common sense and science may both agree that the time process is not reversible. Neither, however, is necessarily committed to the view that there is a reality beyond the process itself. The Christian complicates the matter by introducing the notion of God and, therefore, of an eternal reality beyond the process itself which is supratemporal. There are two ways in which the idea of God may be introduced into the fact of mere process. One is a philosophical argument based on the claim that the changing demands the unchanging, the temporal the eternal, the finite the infinite if the process of becoming is itself to become intelligible. The famous classical proofs are all variations on this same theme. The other source of the idea of God is the discovery by men in their total experience of a reality which exceeds the bounds of sense, a reality which discloses itself in significant events and persons

[1] Goudsmit and Claiborne, op. cit., pp. 166–7.   [2] ibid., p. 168.

and is known as a present reality by later generations when they respond to these events in a certain way, for example by trust and love. In other words, the appeal is to revelation interpreted as an act or acts of disclosure initiated by a reality which transcends the process of becoming: in the Christian case, the living and eternal God. We shall not attempt again to put forth the reasons which seem compelling for a Christian concerning the reality of God. Our problem is how to think and express the relation of the 'eternal' God to the process of change and becoming which our minds have to interpret in temporal terms.

(c) The third question about time, however, demands a brief consideration. The reader will remember the question: does time have a beginning or an end or is it infinite, that is without limit? It is here that we get into the paradoxes. Cullmann has been noted as affirming the infinity of time as the biblical view and thinks we should accept this without further philosophical analysis. Barr is inclined to think that the Bible does not dogmatize on this point. Obviously, if time is clock-time dependent upon the existence of a particular astronomical system, then when the latter disappears, so will time. This was no doubt what was in Augustine's mind when he suggested that the world and time were created together. Unless there is a cosmic process of some kind, some points of reference to a spatial system, it is difficult to see what clock-time could possibly mean. Taking a hint from Bergson, however, we might ask whether duration as the experience of succession and the passage of time could still be meaningful in an environment which is not spatial in the way our present one is. There seems nothing inherently absurd in the idea, except that it is imaginatively inconceivable by us, but not inconceivable in principle as a possibility. The hard-headed empiricist will, of course, say—why bother with a possibility which exceeds all human thought and which can have no practical significance anyhow? The Christian cannot be content with this because he must affirm an Eternal God somehow related to time and if he wants to speak of personal immortality after death, he has to ask what kind of existence this could be which is congruous with the love of God and the reality of personal existence on the other side of death.

Let us sum up briefly our progress so far. Time is real, not simply as a subjective category of thought imposed upon reality by the human mind. It is a feature of the cosmic process as such, which is a process of becoming and change in an irreversible direction. Our particular calendars may be peculiar to our special location in this on-going movement. In this sense, they are man-made. On the other hand, they are not arbitrarily made, but are dictated by configurations of forces in the space-time continuum which are not the result of either human thought or human creative activity. After all, man did not create the solar system. Time is irreversible, a conclusion forced upon us by the present state of scientific knowledge. Until new knowledge of a radically startling kind is available, we must affirm that the arrow of time moves in one direction only. Whether time is infinite, that is endless whether looking to the past or to the future, we will leave undecided until further positions have been considered.

One classical solution to our problem has been to define the eternal as the supra-temporal. But what precisely constitutes the supra-temporal is the crux of the whole matter. As we have already contended, any conception of personal immortality worth the having must for the Christian derive from the prior conviction concerning the reality and nature of God. The mere fact, if such it be, that the 'person' or 'self' survives the present body, is not in itself evidently a good thing. This was argued some years ago now by Professor A. E. Taylor in his Gifford Lectures. He cites two notable instances at the time of his writing which sought to establish immortality without God. One was the appearance of a book by F. W. H. Myers, *Human Personality*, in which empirical, scientific evidence was sought for personal immortality. The other was the effort made by Dr McTaggart to establish personal immortality by metaphysical argument.[1] To both of these attempts, Taylor makes the Christian reply that it is deiformity (that is man's growing into the likeness of God), not mere endless continuance, which is held out to man as the prize of his calling.[2] A similar line of thought is found in the strongly Neoplatonist thought of Dean Inge. Immortality for him is participation in the attributes of the eternal world, namely goodness, truth and beauty. We may still have to use spatial and temporal images as a concession to limitations of thought, but in the last analysis it is quality of life rather than mere continuance which is basic. 'The problem is how to maintain this view of eternity as supra-temporal existence, without either sundering the higher and the lower worlds entirely from each other, or reducing the world of time and change to a vain shadow.'[3] This manner of regarding the problem provides a suitable starting-point

[1] A. E. Taylor, *The Faith of a Moralist*, vol. ii, p. 255.
[2] J. M. E. McTaggart, *Some Dogmas of Religion* and *The Nature of Existence*; C. D. Broad, *An Examination of McTaggart's Philosophy*.
[3] Taylor, op. cit., p. 256.

for a contemporary discussion of this same issue.[1] Dr I. T. Ramsey, like these two earlier thinkers, is concerned to free the notion of personal immortality from a naive conception of the person going on and on in time. In order to do this, he adopts the distinction between sempiternal (that is eternal defined as without beginning or end, existence in a temporal process which is endless, whether viewed from the past or the future) and 'eternal' defined as 'not conditioned by time'.[2] It is worth observing that what Cullmann means by the biblical notion of time is what Ramsey means by sempiternity. The general problem which then arises is: Can we think of eternal or eternity in this second sense (that is not conditioned by time) in any intelligible way which does not interpret it in terms of sempiternity or the sempiternal? Alternatively, and in particular, can we think of eternal life in an intelligible sense which does not think of it as a life 'lasting for ever'?[3] Cullmann would answer this question in the negative on the grounds that the Bible has a view of time which requires us to think of the person going on in time. In fairness to Cullmann, however, it should be acknowledged that for him biblical time is 'filled time', that is time in which God is acting significantly and redemptively for and in man. It is not impossible for Cullmann to argue, therefore, that endless time is not merely temporal succession without quality or spiritual content, since God is for ever active in that temporal succession. If life is meaningful now because our time is filled with the activity of God, there seems to be no reason why a temporal process after death should not acquire a similar or greater meaningfulness because the same God is active in it. Everyone seems to be agreed that we have to use temporal and indeed spatial language, if we are to talk of immortality at all. Ramsey's way of putting it is that all talk of the eternal must be structured by the use of 'models' in the setting of sempiternity. The 'models', taken from the temporal as endlessness, can be developed to a point where a disclosure is made of the nature of the eternal as not conditioned by time. We can never, however, discard the 'models' in the context of sempiternity, as the necessary route by which in experience we arrive at the disclosures of the nature and character of the eternal. The essential point which Ramsey appears to be making is that, just as man is more than his body now, so he is able in present experience to receive a cosmic disclosure of a reality beyond temporal successiveness. Just as the

[1] W. R. Inge, *The Philosophy of Plotinus*, p. 27.
[2] I. T. Ramsey, *The Concept of the Eternal*, Presidential address delivered to the Society for the Study of Theology.   [3] ibid., p. 4.

reality of the 'I' demands more than object-language to indicate its distinctive reality, so human experience requires the recognition of an 'eternal' reality, that is a reality not conditioned by time and space. Here and now we can know ourselves as related to a reality which transcends the temporal. 'So with talk of a future life. "Immortality" tells us of something of which we can be aware here and now; the word belongs to a present disclosure.'[1] Such a disclosure, Dr Ramsey finds, is given in the recognition of duty and our acknowledgement of an absolute obligation to do that duty. As we respond to the moral claim, we here and now experience that claim in the context of a relationship to an 'eternal' reality beyond space and time. This, of course, is not unlike the claim of Kant that, although the pure reason is impotent to arrive at God and therefore, the noumenal, that is reality in itself, the practical reason, through its recognition of the categorical imperative, is able to move from the phenomenal to the noumenal and to postulate the reality of the transcendent God. As we have frequently noted, Christian faith does and must assert the present reality of a relationship to God and, therefore, the present possibility of a foretaste, a down payment, of eternal life. However, to affirm that in disclosures in present experience we are lifted above time and space into a relationship with an eternal realm, not conditioned by space and time, is not quite the same as what the traditional doctrine of personal immortality has wanted to assert. H. D. Lewis has correctly pointed out that it is perfectly possible to talk of a present relationship to an eternal reality and yet not to affirm the full reality of personal existence after death. It may be objected that this is a distinction without a difference. If here and now I can know myself to be in touch with the eternal, then to that extent I participate in an eternal reality and neither the passage of time nor death itself can alter that fact. This is only true to the degree that in my present experience I discover that there is a reality which transcends space and time. It could, however, be interpreted to mean that in the last analysis, it is only that reality which abides, even if all individual persons perish. It must be said again, however, that there is a vast difference between saying that God preserves in His own reality those values which have received partial actualization in my finite, earthly existence and affirming the full reality of personal existence after death. Dr Ramsey makes a strong case for a present experience of eternal life. Somehow he appears to be reluctant to embrace a full-blooded conception of the reality of persons after death as conscious individuals aware of their

[1] I. T. Ramsey, *Freedom and Immortality*, p. 115.

identity as persons. What is the basis of this reluctance? It springs no doubt from the difficulty of conceiving what consciousness, self-awareness and memory could mean in the complete absence of an environment requisite for such self-consciousness. Take away the stream of sensations, perceptions, the constant interaction of our growing personalities with nature and other persons, and how can one give any positive content to what it could mean to be a person under such conditions?

Certainly we have to agree that any intelligible concept of personal immortality requires some kind of environment after death. At the very least there must be a social environment constituted by the other persons who have survived death. But can this make sense unless we assume that such a community of persons is related to some reality equivalent to that of 'nature' in regard to our present experience? Why, however, should it be thought impossible that God could create an environment for persons after death just as He has created one for persons before death? We frankly concede that if the idea of God is completely eliminated, then the question may appear to be purely rhetorical, though there is the case of such philosophers as McTaggart who think that the notion of a community of persons after death without God can be defended on purely metaphysical grounds.

If, however, it is insisted that a doctrine of personal immortality requires an environment of some kind, then the Christian would seem to be left with no option but to assert that God will create such an environment or abandon his belief in the full reality of persons after death. This would appear to be what St Paul does in his famous chapter in I Corinthians. Because God has raised Jesus from the dead, and being who he is, the God of power and love, we can rely on Him to put us after death in the appropriate environment, together with our endowment of a 'spiritual body' suitable for such an existence. He does not spell out in detail exactly how such a life will be lived. Still less does he tackle the philosophical question as to whether he is not committed to the reality of an environment after death for risen believers which must be characterized by something akin to our present space-time world, however distant and remote the analogy may appear to be between heavenly and earthly space and time. To put it simply, he is content to trust God to do what is required to secure the real and meaningful existence of persons in communion with God and their fellows after the death of the individual and of all individuals who have lived or will live in this present physical cosmos. This, it will be said, is the answer to simple faith and does not answer the philosophical difficulties, only evades them. This would only be so if any appeal to God or revelation is declared to be illegitimate, but this is precisely the issue under debate.

We are not saying that faith enables the Christian to describe in detail the nature of 'heavenly space and time', or to give a scientific and philosophical account of the environment created by God for persons after death. We are only saying that such an environment must be postulated, if the Christian faith is true, in order to enable the Christian to speak intelligibly about the relationship of God to persons after death. This latter relationship is, as we have repeatedly admitted, rooted in a present experience in which the character and the nature of the Eternal God is disclosed to us. This means that Ramsey's models, taken in the context of sempiternity, must not be interpreted in such a metaphorical way as to eliminate the temporal element entirely. 'Duration' must be as real for persons after death as it is for us here and now. Granted that the passage of time or successiveness will be vastly different after death from what it is now, we cannot abandon this way of talking without treating persons as only the transient and ephemeral manifestations of an unchanging reality. This would be good Hinduism but it is not the Christian doctrine of personal immortality.

As so often in regard to these deep questions, the late Baron von Hügel has wise words to be heeded. He points out that 'Eternal Life, in a real, though not in the fullest sense, is attributable to man.'[1] Our eternal life is derivative and dependent upon God in a way which must be distinguished from the Eternal Life of the unchanging Godhead. Yet, he goes on to say, our eternal life must have its true form in 'Duration—an ever more or less overlapping succession, capable of being concentrated into quasi-simultaneities.'[2] What does this mean? We have all at one time or another known moments in which the passage of time in the clock sense has been transcended in the intensity of a present experience. Time, as we say, appears to stand still. Whether in the ecstasy of sexual love or the mystic's profound sense of 'union' with God, time as mere successiveness is left behind. This is presumably what von Hügel means by 'quasi-simultaneities'. In our earthly experience, such moments do not last indefinitely and we find ourselves compelled to resume a mode of life in which succession, in the most common-sense meaning of clock-time, once again dominates our thinking and our activities. Note, however, the care with which von Hügel handles this problem. He

[1] F. von Hügel, Eternal Life, p. 383.　　　　　[2] ibid., p. 384.

163

evidently believes that the eternal life of persons after death will involve much more frequent, persistent, and permanent experiences of a relationship to God which transcends time. Nevertheless, he does not eliminate entirely the reality of duration and of some kind of successiveness from such eternal life as will be enjoyed by finite creatures after death. He prefers to talk of 'overlapping succession'. In other words, he tries to combine Dr Ramsey's conception of an eternal life known here and now as a relationship to God which discloses a reality not conditioned by space and time as we know them now, but which retains an element of authentic temporality in the sense of duration for personal existence after death. We believe that this latter element is essential if we want to assert the real existence of persons after death, while asserting that such an existence will involve experiences which transcend clock-time and 'mere' successiveness where 'mere' is the operative word.

This way of putting it seems more satisfactory than that of Professor U. Simon if I understand him correctly. He correctly points out that the 'dimension concept of time makes it impossible for man to envisage an absolute End'.[1] This we have already conceded. But he goes on to say 'God can end time and space, because God is not involved in duration and extension[2].' Presumably, this means that God could bring about the absolute end of the present cosmos.[3] This again is true and most Christians have believed that this will be so. It is quite another question, however, whether God can bring duration and extension in any form to an end and still leave full personal existence to men who are still distinct from their Creator and capable of loving communion with Him. If He can, we cannot understand how this should be so. What the Christian must affirm is the reality of redeemed personal existence in Christ after death, without the destruction of personal individuality. If this can be done by God without the retention of form of environment apprehended in terms of duration and extension, so be it. It would seem impossible, however, for our minds to affirm personal immortality in any full sense on such an assumption. We have no option, therefore, but to take our models, rooted in sempiternity, quite seriously and trust that when we no longer see 'in a glass, darkly', we shall come to understand how man can remain genuinely man after death, while enjoying that unbroken fellowship with God the Father through the Son of which we have been privileged to have a genuine foretaste here and now.

[1] F. von Hügel, *Eternal Life*, p. 384.
[2] U. Simon, *The End is not Yet*, p. 199.　　　　　[3] ibid., p. 199.

In the light of this long and somewhat involved discussion, we confess our view that Christian thinkers should not be too timid in using spatial and temporal 'models' when speaking of personal immortality. This excessive caution is observable even in those thinkers, such as John Knox, who wish to retain a full and rich concept of eternal life in Christ. They are so afraid of the unbridled human imagination filling in the details in a grossly anthropomorphic fashion that they prefer to reduce 'the hope of immortality' to a minimum which soon loses any power to inspire and strengthen. John Knox is perfectly right to say that the Christian hope for the individual is not 'the hope of a simple continuation beyond the grave of his present existence. The life everlasting is not our natural life continuing by its own momentum, as it were, through the specious finality of death'.[1] True enough, though we must remind ourselves that 'our present existence' may be existence 'in Christ'. However, the fact remains that eternal life 'beyond' the grave is not for the Christian merely the prolongation of present physical existence. But it is the real prolongation of the 'person' beyond death, however far-reaching the process of transformation which is being affirmed. If this cannot be affirmed, then we should resolutely drop all talk of personal immortality or of resurrection and frankly believe in God with no hope for personal existence after death. That this is a possible position to take has also been shown to be the case in the early history of the Jews themselves. To imagine that Christians can put the clock back in this sense is impossible. Our faith can and must affirm more than this, for we are the heirs of Christ crucified and risen, and we know in a profounder sense than the early Hebrew that God is not the God of the dead but of the living. This means not only the 'living' here and now but those who have triumphed in Christ over man's last enemy, death, and have passed into the presence of God as His redeemed, reconciled and accepted children. This is not a selfish hope and we cannot be reminded too often, as by John Knox, that the fulfilment of the self can only come to pass in and through community.[2] Community, however, demands real persons, and not merely the preservation in God of disembodied values abstracted from full personal existence. Why should Christians today be content with half a hope instead of the full hope, to realize which Jesus Christ lived, died and rose again?

[1] J. Knox, *Limits of Unbelief*, p. 103.

[2] ibid., p. 105.

Chapter Eleven

Heaven

It follows from all that has been said so far that the ultimate vindication of God's purpose demands an eternal realm if His treatment of all those persons now dead and who will have died before the End is to be reconciled with His love. By 'eternal' here is meant a realm of existence for real persons beyond the world as we now experience it, that is beyond death. We have already contended that such an eternal existence does not necessarily mean one in which time will no longer have any significance for persons in any sense whatsoever. It is not a logical corollary of the assertion that God is timeless that his creatures must be timeless in the same sense. This would only be so if God included the temporal series in Himself. Theism, however, affirms the ontological distinction between Creator and creature. There is no reason in principle on theistic assumptions why this distinction should not also obtain in the life to come. To suggest that for persons after death the experience of 'duration' might still be significant is not to deny the fact that God is timeless.[1] The logic of our argument compels us, therefore, to raise the question of heaven, Dr Robert Jenson rightly points out that 'hope that is not hope for anything is nonsense; the transcendence of a future which is no particular future is as good as no God at all'.[2] J. A. T. Robinson also remarks that 'for a purpose to be cut off at the very instant of achievement would not normally be regarded as fulfilled'.[3] We have opted for real personal existence after death as contrasted with absorption into the Absolute or preservation of the individual only in the 'memory' of God. This, we believe, is the only possible inference from the Christian understanding of God. It also follows that the 'future', whether on this planet or beyond, cannot be completely 'open'. Man is not free to shape any kind of future in complete indifference to or disregard of the will of the transcendent and holy God. The recent modern attacks upon classic

[1] For a discussion of these issues, see H. P. Owen, *Concepts of Deity*.
[2] M. E. Marty and D. G. Peerman, *New Theology*, No. 7, p. 210.
[3] J. A. T. Robinson, *In the End, God*, p. 55.

theology's use of the category of Being as applied to God reveal a fundamental ambiguity. If Being is defined as 'resistant to change' in such a way as to eliminate the freedom of God to act creatively and ever anew in man's history, then obviously it is inadequate to the Bible's understanding of God. On the other hand, God is not free to change His character in and through all the historical changes which man experiences. On this point God is 'resistant to change', otherwise He would cease to be God in the Christian sense. That God is not committed to the preservation of any particular political or cultural *status quo* would seem to be also a plain implication of the Bible's understanding of God, and the way of His working. No earthly order can by definition be permanent between now and the End. In this sense, man's future is radically 'open', but only within the context of God's will. God is radical futurity in that He is working to the establishment of the kingdom which fulfils but transcends history. Until then, we are pilgrims and sojourners and all political and ecclesiastical structures and hopes must submit finally to the gracious but real judgement of God at the End. However, 'faith in the Father's radical temporality, his concrete newness, for the upset of every status quo'[1] cannot be interpreted as the power of God to change His character or to depart from or abandon the purpose of holy love which through Christ will in Christ usher in the final reign of God. The transformation of institutions and social life in this world, important as this is as an essential part of the Christian hope, cannot be a substitute for the hope of the Christian for a real personal and corporate existence in Christ after death and when history has reached its divinely appointed End. Any future historical event cannot by the nature of the case be the fulfilment of the divine purpose unless the earthly kingdom is everlasting and all the dead have a chance to share in it. This means that the vindication of God cannot be only in history, as history is normally understood as a sequence of events determined by the actions of persons in time. In short, this means that the Christian cannot vindicate God by accepting the premises which shape the thinking of agnostics, humanists, Marxists and others for whom this world is the only world there is. The word vindication may cause some problems. Why does God need to be vindicated at all? The basic issue is whether God can be trusted to work consistently towards the goal of the kingdom. To assume that God is either too weak or too unreliable to fulfil His purpose would be in effect to abandon the Christian faith and hope. Since the final kingdom is not yet an

[1] Marty and Peerman, op. cit., p. 213.

established fact for all the reasons we have indicated, the ultimate triumph must be eschatological in the strictest sense, that is at the end of history. Then God's purpose will not only be a hope but be seen to be a genuinely fulfilled hope. Heaven, therefore, is not an addendum tacked on in a casual way to history. It is an integral part of the very conception of God and His purpose which the Bible discloses to us.

If this be so, then we are left with the problem as to how we shall talk of heaven in a manner which gives a reasonably adequate expression to the hope that is in us. There are times when we may be tempted to say of heaven as Augustine said of the Trinity, that we are compelled to speak in order not to be reduced to silence. There are times, no doubt, when silence is the better part of wisdom. Yet even Augustine found it necessary to write at considerable length if Christians were to be grounded and established in the faith. Theologians may have sinned in the past in speaking of heaven in a detailed manner which smacks of a human presumption against which we should be on our guard. Yet to say nothing at all is to leave the Christian mind and imagination a total blank. This is to leave the way open for all kinds of false symbols and superstitious ideas which have little to do with life in Christ. There is no alternative, therefore, but a reverent use of the Christian imagination, respectful of the reticence of Scripture and careful not to go beyond what Christian experience may reasonably demand.

We turn now, therefore, to the problems of language and symbol in our talk of the after-life: how shall we speak of the resurrection life and of heaven? It is not enough to say that because no man has been to 'heaven' and returned that we are in no position to say anything about it. If the Christian enjoys a real foretaste of 'eternal life' here and now, then he knows that life in Christ hereafter is not totally different from the life he knows now, if one is thinking in terms of our relationship to God, our dependence upon Him, the enjoyment of fellowship with Him, the social bonds of love which unite all who are in Christ. The fruits of the Spirit will be as meaningful there as here. The resurrection life is not the translation of the Christian into a mode of life which is totally different, in the moral and spiritual order, from the fellowship he now enjoys with God through Christ and with his fellow-believers.

In another sense, of course, it will be, as we have insisted, a very different kind of existence. The very fact that death is behind him instead of in front of him is a crucial difference. Time and space will not be the same, but we do not have to assume that our present experience of space and time is the only form which such an experience can take. This being the case, it is clear that we can only speak of this aspect of the resurrection life in symbolic terms, that is with images and language taken from present experience, together with the recognition that the symbols cannot be perfectly adequate to the reality of this resurrection life. In view of the ambiguity and confusion which attaches to the word 'myth', it is better not to say that we must talk of the after-life in mythical terms. Even the word 'symbol' could be misleading if symbol is taken to mean mere metaphor which does not point to reality, or if it suggests mere imagination and human artifice. Story and parable are equally ambiguous unless one faces the question as to whether the story points to some truth about the reality of the resurrection life. Modesty here is in order, provided it does not lead us into sheer and total agnosticism. There is much that the Christian cannot know in detail about life after death. It cannot be true for the Christian that he does not know anything at all. He knows God; he knows Christ; he lives now in the fellowship of the Spirit with other believers. This may leave him with many unanswered questions. It does not leave him with a total mental blank as to the kind of life in Christ to which he may look forward after death.

When all is said and done, however, it may be urged that the very idea of continued existence 'in Christ' after death presents a picture of eternal boredom which is intolerable, if taken seriously. This is in part due to the fact that symbols taken from sight rather than from action have tended to dominate in the classical descriptions of heaven. In the ancient Catholic tradition of the vision of God (the *visio Dei*), where the fullness of eternal life is conceived after the analogy of seeing or beholding, this is particularly true. Where contemplation in this sense is central, then it is the aesthetic enjoyment, the beholding of God in all the beauty of His holiness which becomes the heart of the experience of God in the resurrection life. When, however, the aesthetic symbols become completely dominant to the exclusion of other ways of speaking, there are obvious difficulties. The contemplation of beauty does demand a certain detachment, a standing at a distance to be able to take in and appreciate the picture as a whole. Though our feelings are involved when we look at a picture, it would be a straining of language to see in the aesthetic relationship an adequate symbol of the complex depths of love, whether between God and man or between persons. From the Christian point of view, the experience of God after death must involve not only admiration from a distance but active love between God and His children. Yet how can we express this? Surely only by a careful use of images taken from inter-personal relationships here below and especially our relationship to Jesus Christ, and as a consequence our new relationship to our fellow-men.

But what shall we 'do' in heaven? Does not even the prospect of eternal loving open up the possibility of eternal boredom? It has to be recognized that this problem of boredom is not peculiar to whatever kind of life we believe to exist after death. It is obviously a danger, or even a reality, in this life. Men and women here below get bored with each other and sometimes with sex itself. They go about with unseeing eyes when the world is full of the beauty of the changing seasons. We all know 'good' people, that is morally self-disciplined people, who are frightfully dull. This makes us sometimes prefer the company of pagans on the mistaken grounds that it is their paganism which makes them more interesting and exciting. And, of course, there is the dull, mechanized routine of daily life in a highly industrialized and technological society. About this, however, two things are to be observed. Few people are so bored as to be ready to commit suicide to escape from it all. Secondly, most people at some time in their lives have experiences which are so fulfilling and so intrinsically worth while that it never occurs to them to ask whether they are bored or not, Love, friendship, beauty, the fashioning of new truth and beauty, whether with hand or brain—these things satisfy in such a profound sense that it never occurs to us to ask whatever God there be to save us from the repetition of such experiences. Perhaps repetition is itself a misleading word, since there is both variety and sameness in what are similar experiences. To put it bluntly, if we are bored with love, life, beauty, worship, this is not because there is a continuity and even a sameness about our experiences of these things, but because of our selfishness, lust and distorted sense of values; in fact, because of our sin.

Yet, say some, will not all excitement disappear when sin and evil are no longer there to be fought? Must not the negative always exist to show up the positive? As a possibility, perhaps, but surely not in the realm of fact. Must hate always exist as reality in order to make love meaningful? Must ugliness always be part of the picture before beauty can be appreciated? Can truth never shine in its own light apart from error? That this is so in our present experience does not make it intrinsically so. Yet it does mean that in our language about heaven, we must find room for creativity, for symbols of meaningful activity. 'My Father worketh hitherto, and I work.'[1] If God is essentially Creator and we are endowed with some measure of His creative power and initiative, then Christians can reasonably believe that life in heaven will be active. That we cannot spell out in detail the nature of these activities does not make the notion absurd. It is enough for the Christian to know that heaven will be more, not less, gloriously a place of meaningful and creative action than even this present world. More than this we do not need to know at this stage of our pilgrimage. On the basis of his present knowledge of God, mediated through the life, death and resurrection of Jesus Christ and experienced now in the Spirit in the fellowship of believers, the Christian may look forward to a glorious personal immortality. This may be an 'embodied' existence, provided this is not taken to mean the continuance of the present physical body. Whether we talk of personal immortality or the resurrection of the body matters little, provided the previous points are understood and taken fully into account. Because such a doctrine of personal immortality emphasizes the existence of individual persons after death, it is not a selfish hope. Since it is life in Christ, it must by the nature of the case involve community, the life of persons in relationship. Individuality as selfishness is transcended, but not individuality as the reality of personal existence. To destroy the latter is to destroy the very possibility of love and is at the same time a rejection of the kind of God in whom the Christian most profoundly believes. We may see in a glass, darkly, as far as this present life is concerned, but it was surely never the intention of St Paul to suggest that we can see nothing at all. 'Seeing', of course, is another metaphor when used of the spiritual life. The fact remains that we have known and experienced now the love of the Eternal God, and divine light has been shed abroad in our hearts. Why should the Christian opt for anything less than the full hope? In doing so, he will find his energies quickened for a more dedicated service in this world. He will be concerned for the welfare of the whole man here and now because He knows that God cares for men now and in eternity.

[1] John 5: 17 A.V.

Chapter Twelve

Down to Earth Again

The fundamental thesis of this book has been that the Christian hope is a two-tiered one—a hope for this world and for personal immortality of an 'embodied' kind after death. The prospect for the Christian believer is not an 'either-or' but a 'both-and'. However unbalanced some aspects of the Christian tradition have been, Christians can have the best of both worlds in a more than superficial sense. This present world, despite sin and evil, is God's world. We have been set in it to do the Heavenly Father's will. Nor are we justified in setting prior limits to what God can do with this world, given the responsive faith of men and the continuing grace of God. This being so, there can be on the part of the Christian no premature despair of this world. On the other hand, whatever our talk about the God of the future, of man's openness for the future and similar language, we have argued that there is no theology of hope in the full Christian sense which ignores the problem of death and the ultimate destiny of the individual. A hope for the future which excludes the vast majority of the human race from the possibility of personal spiritual fulfilment and from sharing in the abundant life promised is a bogus hope. A life of genuine personal existence after death is, therefore, a necessary implication of the Christian faith in a God of holy love. Whatever the problems connected with the use of imagery and symbol to express that conviction, the conviction is important and without it the gospel is no longer the good news about a salvation which death cannot touch.

Christian faith must, therefore, be opposed to any kind of utopianism—liberal, humanist, socialist, Marxist, technological, scientific—which excludes most of the human race from the chance of personal fulfilment and from participation in whatever ideal future is envisaged. We have frankly acknowledged that the Christian convictions about life after death depend upon the recovery of faith in God in the full Christian sense. They are not dependent upon psychical research or demonstrative philosophical argument. It is highly unlikely that, in the foreseeable future, men in the West are going to recover confidence in a life after death worth the having on the basis of philosophical arguments, whether of the Platonic or the McTaggart variety. In the East, the context of the question is different. Karma involves survival interpreted in terms of metempsychosis, but it cannot in its present form satisfy the aspirations of men, even in the Eastern world. Nirvana does justice neither to man's hope for this world nor for a satisfying personal existence beyond death. It also seems inevitable that both Hinduism and Buddhism will increasingly experience the crisis of belief provoked by the widespread secularism of our time. If secular man objects to metaphysical arguments in favour of theism in its Western form, it is not probable that he will more readily accept the same kind of reasoning in favour of karma or reincarnation.

To return, however, to the theme of this chapter—'down to earth again'—we must confront directly a question which has no doubt been in the reader's mind from the beginning. Granted, he might say, the truth of what you say about personal immortality of an embodied kind, I would still like to know how you envisage the immediate future of the human race and its long-term prospects on this planet. Surely you are not suggesting at this stage of history that we should retire into the desert as anchorites or contract out of our responsibilities à la hippie, or even enter a monastery? What does the Christian propose to do about the world now? This is fair comment and we shall attempt some kind of answer, remembering that an adequate reply would demand another book or many books.

In an age when solutions to all our problems tend to be sought in grandiose schemes for social reconstruction, the first point to be made is that the Christian, by virtue of his loyalty to Christ, is compelled to seek for the expression of love to his neighbour in personal attitude and behaviour. He is called to show love to individual men and women he meets, not to love the abstraction 'mankind'. This is true even when we are dealing with such complex issues as poverty, injustice, race and war. This needs to be emphasized since it is very easy to support idealistic social schemes without the compassionate sympathy and friendliness which is one mark at least of Christian behaviour. We have all known some social idealists who are constantly uttering tirades against poverty but who have never befriended a poor person, still less have chosen to share his lot. There are even some high-minded people who will reject the tramp's appeal for immediate help on the grounds that they are working for a new social order in which the tramp will be abolished. Not all who speak so glibly about racial equality are conspicuous in their loving and friendly attitude to people who differ from them in colour. Proponents of social justice are not always averse to the status and advantages which money brings. They send their children to expensive schools and colleges. In England, some accept seats in the House of Lords. In the USA some accept high office and position with all the perquisites they bring. We are not sitting in judgement or even suggesting that there is something unChristian in seeking the best education for one's children. There is, however, something nauseating about the kind of idealism which indulges in romantic dreams about the total transformation of the social order and is curiously indifferent to the actual men and women who live in it now. The Christian is called upon to show love, sympathy and compassion now when and where he can. Blueprints for a perfect, sinless society are no substitutes for immediate expressions of Christian love. Slogans such as 'we want justice, not charity' do not affect this point. Passionate political arguments in favour of higher old-age pensions are no substitute for visiting old people and befriending them in what may be the loneliest part of their lives. Man lives not by bread alone, and old people know this very well. The Christian is called first of all to love the people he actually meets, however, dirty, unpleasant and repellent. Some will begin to scream that this is the old deception of 'pie in the sky', the blunting of misery to persuade the deprived of seeking their just rights in this world. The reply to this is 'Nonsense!' People are people, not ciphers in some grand abstraction of a social order. It will be a betrayal of the Christian gospel if we ever forget this. It will be a sad day for the world when compassion, sympathy and personal love and consideration are banished in the name of whatever human utopia and replaced by social reformers, planners and welfare administrators.

It also needs to be said that Christianity is not responsible for the totality of evil in the world. To hear some people speak today, one would imagine that lust and pride and selfishness were not in the world until Christianity came into it. There is still too much of the half-baked philosophy of Rousseau in the modern world, with the naive assumption that when the last king has been strangled in the entrails of the last priest, then man's natural innocence and purity will assert itself. Or to be really modern, when the last capitalist has been strangled in the entrails of the last of the bourgeoisie. This, of course, is ridiculous. When the Church and individual Christians have been castigated for their sins and failures throughout the ages, the fact remains that much of the evil in the world is the direct result of the sinfulness of men. It is a convenient excuse to blame the Church for my egoism, but it will not work. If all that has been said in criticism of the Church were true, it would still remain a fact that man's chief problem is himself, and this is not an invention of the Christians. Nor is it possible to infer that if all Christians perfectly exemplified the spirit of their Lord, then all our problems would automatically disappear. There is not a shred of evidence in the New Testament to suggest that men will necessarily respond to the gospel. If the Church here and now were the perfect and unspotted Bride of Christ, she might very well suffer crucifixion and martyrdom rather than universal acceptance. The idea that Christians have some magic wand which, when waved, will immediately transform the world into the kingdom is neither Christian nor sensible. If this were so, there would have been no need for the life, death and resurrection of Jesus Christ in the first place. All this, which will no doubt provoke angry reaction in some, needs to be said with the utmost vigour in order to cut through the miasma of sentimentalism which surrounds this subject. Christians cannot of themselves change the world as a whole. Only God could do that, and He has chosen to do it by the slow operation of suffering love which leaves men their freedom and responsibility. There are many people in the world today who want the Church to create a new and ideal world but are themselves quite unwilling to accept the fact of their own sin and responsibility, or to accept the spiritual cost of being willing to submit to a transformation of their own lives by the Spirit of God which is love. There is much to be said for the view that the real Pharisees in the world today are not to be found only or primarily in the churches but in those complacent social idealists and reformers who are so sure of themselves and of their intentions. They are so confident in themselves, in their answers to every human problem, so convinced that if only their schemes were adopted, the new world would come overnight. All previous generations have had to fight the demons of lust, pride and love of power. Not so these new Pharisees who are convinced that they are not as other men are. They have been born in original righteousness rather than original sin. Only previous generations have shown their weakness and folly in the struggle against evil. Now the 'new man' has appeared who sees through it all. It has always been a temptation to locate the source of evil in an individual or group of individuals other than oneself or one's group. Hitler located it in the Jews, some whites locate it in the coloured and some coloured in the white, the non-communist in the communist and vice-versa. One could go on to give an indefinite list. There is no hope for the world until all men, no matter who they are, acknowledge their common sinfulness, imperfection and prejudice. The black is just as capable of violence, injustice, pride and snobbery as the white. The Marxist is no more free from the lust of personal power than the capitalist. The young person is just as open as his father before him to the corrupting influences of self-interest in all his attempts to live by the perfect law of love. Even in the delicate area of women power, there is no guarantee that women will exercise power more humanely than men when they get it. Some of the most unpleasant characters in history have been women as well as men. As long as any group, whoever they may be, regard themselves as the embodiment of truth, enlightenment, progress, etc. no real human community, based on the truth about ourselves, is possible. There remains only the arbitrament of violence and force and this is precisely what we are getting in increasing measure in our contemporary Western society.

All this needs to be said again and again, and a Christianity which shirks this unpleasant task is a salt which has lost its taste. Much can be said about the failures of Christians and churches and they must constantly remind themselves that judgement begins with the house of God. It is important, however, that Christians should not allow their own confession of sin to give the impression that all other men are thereby rendered pure. The Christian has to remind all men, including himself, that they and he are accountable to a holy God, that all have sinned and fallen short of the glory of God, that no man is a perfect instrument and embodiment of the cause which he has espoused. Without this true self-knowledge, all our social idealism is built upon a lie because it presupposes a doctrine of man which is not grounded in the facts of history and experience. No social order, however progressive and enlightened, can generate the kind of active love for the neighbour of which we have been speaking. This is the fruit of a direct relationship to Jesus Christ, and from Him alone can come the kind of love which is free from condescension to the neighbour and from a subtle form of self-righteousness which makes some forms of 'Christian' love so unlovely.

Having said this, however, what can the Christian do more than seek to express the love of Christ on the level of immediate personal relationships? What should he do *vis-à-vis* the power structures of any particular society, embodied in political and economic institutions? Various attitudes have been manifest in the long course of Christian history and we shall list them in turn in order to see more clearly what the issues are.

(*a*) The Christian should have nothing to do with politics at all. This is part of the larger issue as to whether the Christian should take a negative or a positive attitude to the cultural situation in which he finds himself. Richard Niebuhr has given us a brilliant analysis of the problems which arise in this connection.[1] We agree that it is not possible to solve this question by a simple appeal to the attitudes of the early Christians as evidence in the New Testament. The strength of their eschatological hopes and their presence in a pagan society where there was little or no possibility of peaceful constitutional change in the social order make it impossible for us to use this period as a basis for our answers to the question of the Christian's involvement. However, it must be said that this judgement is itself relevant mainly to the societies which enjoy some degree of political democracy. In some parts of the world, Christians find themselves in much the same situation as obtained in the Roman Empire. Karl Barth offended a lot of Christians in the West some years ago when he pointed out that this was the situation of the Christian Church in Hungary. We discovered then that it was very easy for Christians to 'talk big' to their fellow Christians when there was no danger of their being called upon to back up their talk with costly suffering and personal sacrifice. It is obviously important, therefore, to distinguish between situations where the Christian has open to him the means of peaceful social change and where he does not have this option.

(*b*) There are situations in the modern world where peaceful change in political and economic institutions seems remote or well-nigh impossible: China, Russia, Cuba, the Russian satellites, South America, South Africa, some African states, Arab sheikdoms. This list is not based only on prejudice. Of course it is true that, even in these countries, the rulers have to take some account of public opinion. We are all aware these days that in Russia there are trends critical of the present regime among artists, intellectuals and some religious sects. Not even in China can there be absolute universal conformity to the thoughts of Chairman Mao. Not all South American states can be lumped together under one descriptive category-tyranny. Some of the one-party states in Africa permit some freedom of opinion and its expression, while lacking any permitted channels of a formal constitutional kind through which this opinion can manifest itself as a claim to an alternative form of government. The shades of grey are

[1] R. R. Niebuhr, *Christ and Culture.*

almost infinitely varied. The fact, remains that, on the whole, these countries do not have guaranteed constitutional means for political and social change.

The most urgent ethical problem which confronts Christians in these countries, as indeed elsewhere, is whether they can countenance the violent overthrow of existing regimes in the name of Christ. For the Marxist, no such moral dilemma emerges. For him, the use of force is a matter of strategy and of correct timing. It is not a matter of principle. This, however, can never be the case for the Christian. When it is asked today—what are you Christians willing to do in these situations?—there is no simple blanket answer. There is no way in which the leaders in the institutional churches can free the individual Christian from the agonizing responsibility of deciding what the will of God for him is under a particular set of circumstances. The Christian pacifist can, perhaps, give an answer which for him at any rate is consistent and universally applicable. No violence at any time under any circumstances. For the Christian who is not a pacifist, no such clear-cut answer is possible. He has to wrestle with each situation and each predicament as it arises. Dr Ernest Payne, in a notable address to the Protestant Dissenting Deputies on March 17, 1971, has no difficulty in showing that some Christians in the past have been willing to risk the use of force to bring about necessary social change.[1] He is not saying that force is 'good' in any absolute sense, still less that it is the will of God that men should use violence as God's method of dealing with human problems. I understand him to be saying that in some circumstances, the Christian has little option but to decide on a course of action which he knows to be 'wrong' if judged in the light of God's absolute holy love. In other words, the Christian must sometimes knowingly 'sin' if sin is defined as acting in a manner which falls short of the absolute will of God interpreted as agape-love without qualification. This, of course, is true of all Christians every day and in every place. All have sinned and all have come short of the glory of God. It is no doubt this element of moral 'compromise' which led the late Aldous Huxley to speak as he did in the interesting passage quoted by Dr Payne. 'Religion can have no politics except the creation of small-scale societies of chosen individuals outside and on the margins of the essentially unviable large-scale societies, whose nature dooms them to self-frustration and suicide.'[2] However, as Payne rightly says, though such withdrawal from participation seems on the surface to be more Christian, in fact it is an unChristian refusal

[1] E. A. Payne, *Violence, Non-Violence and Human Rights.*   [2] ibid., p. 14.

to accept our mutual involvement with the problems of sinful men on the specious plea that it is better for the Christian to retain his purity of conscience, even if this means isolation from his sinful fellowmen. Another contemporary who has wrestled with this problem is Jacques Ellul.[1] Like Huxley, though from different premises, Ellul believes that 'the world is radically, totally evil', and it remains totally evil after the Incarnation.[2] This means that the Christian can fight with violence for social justice in the name of Christ. If he does this, let him do it in full awareness. The important thing is that when he uses violence, the Christian knows very well 'that he is doing wrong, is sinning against the God of love'.[3] He must submit himself to God's judgement and hope for His grace and forgiveness. Further, the Christian must be the 'conscience' of any movement he joins and not shrink from criticizing in the name of Christ those who are victorious in the social revolution. That is, he must recognize that men are never morally pure, whatever side they are on in any social conflict.

(c) There are other situations, however, where freedom to pursue political change is possible. This is largely true in those nations which have adopted some form of political democracy after the Western model. It is true of the Western states in the main, even if the radicals insist that the USA is tyrannical to its rebels like every other society. No society on earth is a perfect democracy. The situation is never a simple black or white but always a grey. None the less, there are significant differences between respective societies. Because all societies are imperfect and sinful, it does not follow that it is a matter of indifference which kind of society we have. Very dubious sentiments were expressed in this regard during the last war. Some suggested that because the motives of the Allies were not entirely pure, therefore there was no justification for preferring democratic institutions to Nazism. Because the struggle was not a simple battle between pure good and unmitigated evil, therefore it was improper to make any moral judgements at all about the respective merits of the two causes. This, however, is an impossible position to take. It could result in complete passivity which would be a denial of responsibility, or it could issue in capitulation to political reaction of the worst kind. It is equivalent to saying that because all Christians are sinners and not yet perfect men and women, therefore we have no right at all to do battle for good causes.

Nevertheless, I believe that many Christians, who are not socially reactionary, are deeply concerned about giving Christian sanction to

[1] J. Ellul, *Violence*.   [2] ibid., pp. 25–6.   [3] ibid., pp. 137–8.

violence in a society where violence is becoming increasingly endemic. It is all very well to talk of the use of force in the interests of social justice and to use high-sounding language about the Christian being the 'conscience' of the movements he supports. The Christian needs to be very realistic at this point. If he supports the unleashing of violence, he must face the fact that once it starts, he will have little or no control over the consequences. Christians are bound to be a minority in any such movement, and it is very improbable that in the change of power those who come out on top will be Christian or even 'sympathetic' to Christian values. A Christian may still feel that under certain conditions, he is right to take the risk. He should, however, do it with his eyes open and not fool himself that the resulting revolution will not also bring its own injustices. If his Christian conscience still says that the risk is justified, so be it.

This issue cuts very deep and it is not going to be easy. James Klugmann quotes with approval a statement of Karl Marx to the effect that 'By acting on the world and changing it, man changes his own nature.'[1] If this means that the change of political and economic structures produces a radical change in human nature, then one can only marvel at the naiveté of Marx and those who follow him. Can we really substantiate this astonishingly optimistic view of social change from the history of France, Russia, China and Cuba within the memories of most of us? Are we seriously expected to believe that a 'new man' has really been produced? Whatever other merits these great social revolutions may have, the radical transformation of human nature is hardly one of them. Klugmann protests against some kinds of Christian criticism which imply that Marxists are too hopeful and too optimistic. Some Christians may use this criticism because of their cynical disbelief in any kind of social progress. Nevertheless, the criticism is correct. The Marxist's hope is incredible if he really believes that human nature can be changed in this way. Note that the Marxist's naiveté does not consist in the fact that he sees the necessity for a new type of man and woman, but in the way in which he thinks this can be brought about. The Christian does not or ought not to deny the premise that men and women can be changed at the deepest levels of attitude and behaviour. What he must question is that social change in the Marxist, or indeed in any other merely sociological sense, can in fact bring about this change in people. The only power in history which has shown itself capable of transforming persons in a more than superficial sense has been religion. We say religion, because

[1] *The Christian Hope*, S.P.C.K. Theological Collections 13, p. 61.

this is not exclusively true of Christianity alone. Hindu and Buddhist have developed ways of changing human consciousness and men's scale of values. This, however, has never been brought about by social change in the modern secular sense. It has been the consequence of a deep religious commitment which goes far beyond the limits of any kind of sociology, Marxist or otherwise.

Let us now return to our basic question concerning the Christian attitude to social change in the light of the conviction that men are invited by God to share with Him and with each other a blessed existence after death. It is obviously impossible to deal exhaustively with such vast issues in the final chapter of a book devoted in the main to other questions. The reader is reminded again of the perspective from which these problems will be considered.

The ultimate goal of the Christian life is the personal and corporate fulfilment of mankind in a realm beyond space and time as we know them. In this sense, Christianity, with its allied notions of personal immortality and of the redeemed community beyond death and present history, is other-worldly. It rejects any form of utopian idealism which makes the ultimate hope a perfect human society on earth. On the other hand, it does not and cannot agree with the Feuerbachian dictum that 'where the heavenly life is a truth, there the earthly life is a lie'.[1] The reason why the Christian does not have to take a merely negative attitude to this world is that he has already experienced the power of the grace of God to change men and women in this life. Because this is for him not only a possibility but a fact, it follows that if men can be made new, if only in part, this world and its institutions can also reflect such newness. The possibility of the transformation of society is at least admitted in principle. There are, however, definite limits here which both Christian faith and social realism compel us to acknowledge. If progress is defined in purely external terms, namely technological mastery of environment and the more adequate satisfaction of the physical needs of men, then it is no doubt possible to envisage something like a continuous and ever advancing progress. If, however, progress is defined in terms of love of truth, moral integrity, compassion or agape-love, it is obvious that a new generation does not start off where the previous one finished. When all has been said about the influence of family, social environment and cultural inheritance, the fact remains that each generation has to receive, assimilate and personally actualize again the intellectual, moral and spiritual values it has received. Christian, agnostic or Marxist parents

[1] H. Gollwitzer, *The Christian Faith and the Marxist Criticism of Religion*, p. 52.

do not infallibly guarantee children of the same loyalties and persuasions. Christian fathers may have atheistic sons, agnostic fathers may have believing sons, Marxist fathers may have believing children (witness the remarkable example of Stalin's daughter). We are in no way denying the immensely powerful influences of family and social environment, but we are saying that there is no way in which one generation can guarantee the same loyalties and values in the generation which follows. There is no inheritance of acquired characteristics in the intangible realm of values. This simple fact is often ignored completely in discussion of the future and our hope for the future. Each generation has its own inalienable freedom and responsibility. Each generation in the last analysis chooses its own loyalties. This is why progress in more than a superficial sense is not a continuous straight line. This is why history is a story of progress and retrogressions, a fact so unpalatable to all framers of grandiose philosophies of history. In this sense, history is 'open', but for better or for worse. This is what makes any kind of facile utopianism impossible, even if one were not a Christian.

It may be objected that if this is the case, it is as fatal to any Christian philosophy of history as it is to any of the humanist or Marxist versions. The charge may well be admitted if the term 'philosophy of history' implies a deterministic inevitability about history, whether the inevitability be the result of a predestinating divine decree or the Marxist dialectic. The Christian bases his confidence for the future on the triumphs of the divine love in the past and in the present. If God can transform the cross of Jesus Christ into a source of spiritual power, then we may hope and believe that no arbitrary limits can be set to what such love can achieve in the future, whether on this earth or beyond it. The Christian may hold such a hope in faith. He cannot 'know' in advance how all men will react between now and the end of human history. In all his dreams for the final kingdom, he knows that God, by His own decision, will have to reckon with the incalculable freedom of men and their potential disobedience and rebellion. Hope and realism are inextricably combined in the Christian faith, and there is no escaping from this fact. 'If, in Nietzsche's words, idealism is defined as the inability to bear the truth about man, then Christian faith is much less idealistic than Marxism.'[1]

The Christian, therefore, is called upon to maintain a delicate balance between an extreme pessimism, which reflects a lack of trust in the power of the divine love and a foolish optimism which has not

[1] H. Gollwitzer, *The Christian Faith and the Marxist Criticism of Religion*, p. 123.

yet considered the 'weight of sin' in human affairs. It is so much easier to occupy either one of these two extremes. When this is done, then the resulting interpretation of history becomes more neat and tidy, even if it is the neatness of a negative pessimism. But history is not and never has been neat and tidy in this sense. Certainly God is a God of order and not of disorder and the Christian looks forward to the victory of moral and spiritual order over disorder at the End. This divine order, however, has to be won in the face of man's stubborn self-will and as far as human history is concerned, the way to resurrection passes inevitably through the Cross. 'No Cross, no Crown', as the early Puritans used to say.

It has been the thesis of this book that modern Christians must recover a strong confidence in God and the reality of personal immortality as the destiny which God wills for His children, unless they deliberately refuse it. Austin Farrer's comment is in our view thoroughly justified: 'There are people now who profess the Christian name, and who are nevertheless ashamed of heavenly hope. The cry is raised, "A this worldly religion". There may be a bonus hereafter—only better not count on it. But I tell you that Christianity cannot for any length of time survive the amputation of such a limb as life to come.'[1] It is also part of our thesis that the above convictions do not mean a retreat into a false other-worldliness which despises earth or our role here and now in shaping our earthly future, but it does involve a realism about future possibilities which is not cynicism. We have not attempted in this chapter to outline a programme of Christian action for the future. This would require another book and would at this stage only distract the reader from the facing of the issues which we have previously raised. There will no doubt be some who will see in our thesis what could superficially be dubbed Christian pessimism. This is not so. A realistic assessment of the realities of human sin has always been considered pessimistic by those who have not experienced the grace of God. Teilhard De Chardin has asked the searching question as to whether the human race, once it has really come of age intellectually, will not fall victim to hopeless despair and throw in the sponge. It is hardly enough to reply to this that it is ridiculous, that sheer animal vitality will keep the human race going. It is a modern myth that heaven is a distraction from earth, and therefore a hindrance and an obstacle to real social progress. It may in fact turn out to be the case that man can never enjoy earth in its fullness without the recovery of a strong belief in the reality of heaven. At least this is

[1] A. Farrer, *A Celebration of Faith*, p. 165.

what Christian faith confesses. For to believe in heaven is to believe in the compassionate God and Father of our Lord Jesus Christ who will not abandon His children, even in the valley of the shadow. This confidence and this alone can free men to enjoy the earth and work for the fullest possible human existence here and now without tasting the inevitable bitterness and frustration of a hope which rests entirely on an earthly bliss which by its very nature must be transient. For the Christian, it is not an 'either-or' but a 'both-and': this world and the world to come. Thus we can look forward with hope—a hope which has faith in the power of God to change persons in the future, and thus to make earth a nearer approximation to heaven. To this, however, must be added the ultimate hope that man's last enemy, death, has been conquered and that our final home is that 'eternal city' whose builder and maker is God.

Bibliography

The literature on this subject is enormous, and no attempt is made here to give an exhaustive list or even to include all good books concerned with this theme. The present list contains all books cited in the text, together with other suggestions for reading for the interested student who may wish to pursue certain topics in greater detail. Those who wish a more popular and less technical approach should start with those books marked with an asterisk.

Altizer, T. J. J. and Hamilton, W.   *Radical Theology and the Death of God* Bobbs-Merrill, New York, 1966)

Augustine, St.   *Confessions* (Dent Everyman, London, 1929)

Baillie, J.   *And the Life Everlasting* (Oxford U.P., London, 1936)

Barbour, I. G.   *Issues in Science and Religion* (S.C.M., London, 1968)

Barr, J.   *Biblical Words for Time* (S.C.M., London, 1962)
   Old and New in Interpretation (S.C.M., London, 1966)

Baum, G.   *Man Becoming* (Herder & Herder, Billingshurst, 1970)

Benoit, P. and Murphy, R.   *Immortality and Resurrection* (Herder & Herder, Billingshurst, 1970)

Bevan, E.   *Symbolism and Belief* (Allen & Unwin, London, 1938)

Bonhoeffer, D.   *Ethics*, ed. E. Bethge (S.C.M., London, 1955)

Boros, L.   *The Moment of Truth* (Burns & Oates, London, 1962)

Borst, C. V. (ed.)   *The Mind/Brain Identity Theory* (Macmillan, London, 1970)

Broad, C. D.   *An Examination of McTaggart's Philosophy* (Cambridge U.P., 1938)

Bultmann, R.   *History of the Synoptic Tradition*, tr. J. Marsh (Blackwell, Oxford, 1963)
   Theology of the New Testament, vols i, ii (S.C.M., London, 1952)

Campbell, C. A.   *On Selfhood and Godhood* (Allen & Unwin, London, 1957)

Chardin, T. De   *The Future of Man* (Collins, London, 1964)
   The Phenomenon of Man (Collins, London, 1961)

Choron, J.   *Death and Western Thought* (Collier, New York, 1963)

Clark, N.   *Interpreting the Resurrection* (S.C.M., London, 1967)

Cobb, J. B. (Jr)   *A Christian Natural Theology* (Westminster, Philadelphia, 1965)

Cohn, N.   *The Pursuit of the Millennium* (Paladin, London, 1970)

Cox, H.   *The Secular City* (Macmillan, New York, 1965)

Cullmann, O. *Christ and Time*, tr. F. V. Filson (S.C.M., London, 1962)
  Immortality of the Soul or Resurrection of the Body? (Epworth, London, 1958)
  Salvation in History (S.C.M., London, 1967
  The Early Church (S.C.M., London, 1966)
Dahl, M. E. *The Resurrection of the Body*, Studies in Biblical Theology No. 36 (S.C.M., London, 1962)
Edwards, D. L. *Religion and Change* (Hodder & Stoughton, London, 1969)
  The Last Things Now (S.C.M., London, 1969)
Ellul, J. *Violence* (S.C.M., London, 1970)
Evans, C. F. *Resurrection and the New Testament*, Studies in Biblical Theology, Second Series No. 12, (S.C.M., London, 1970)
Farrer, A. *A Celebration of Faith* (Hodder & Stoughton, London, 1970)
  Saving Belief (Hodder & Stoughton, London, 1964)
  The Freedom of the Will (A. & C. Black, London, 1957)
Findlay, J. N. *Hegel* (Allen & Unwin, London, 1958)
Flew, A. (ed.) *Body, Mind and Death* (Collier-Macmillan, London, 1964)
Garaudy, R. *Marxism in the Twentieth Century* (Collins, London, 1970)
Gatch, M. McC. *Death-Meaning and Mortality in Christian Thought and Contemporary Culture* (Seabury Press, New York, 1969)
George, R. *Communion with God* (Epworth, London, 1953)
Gibson, J. Boyce *Theism and Empiricism* (S.C.M., London, 1970)
Gilkey, L. *Naming the Whirlwind: The Renewal of God Language* (Bobbs-Merrill, New York, 1969)
Gollwitzer, H. *The Christian Faith and the Marxist Criticism of Religion* (St Andrew Press, Edinburgh, 1970)
Goudsmit, S. A. and Claiborne, R. *Time* (Time-Life International, Nederland, N.V., 1970)
Hanson, A. T. (ed.) *Vindications* (S.C.M., London, 1966)
Heidegger, M. *Being and Time*, tr. J. Macquarrie & E. Robinson, (Blackwell, Oxford, 1979)
Herzog, F. *The Future of Hope: Theology as Eschatology* (Herder & Herder, Billingshurst, 1970)
Hick, J. *Christianity at the Centre* (S.C.M., London, 1968)
  Evil and the God of Love (Collins Fontana, London, 1970
Houghton, W. E. *The Victorian Frame of Mind* 1830–70 (Yale U.P., New Haven, 1957)
Hoyle, F. *The Nature of the Universe* (Blackwell, Oxford, 1950)
Hügel, F. von *Eternal Life* (T. & T. Clark, Edinburgh, 1948)
Inge, W. R. *Outspoken Essays*, Second Series (Longmans, London, 1927)
  The Philosophy of Plotinus (Longmans, London, 1929)
Joad, C. E. M. *Guide to Modern Thought* (Faber, London, 1948)
  Guide to Philosophy (Gollancz, London, 1936)
Kaufman, G. *Systematic Theology: A Historicist Perspective* (Scribner, New York, 1968)

Knox, J.   *Limits of Unbelief* (Collins, London, 1970)

Lamont, C.   *The Illusion of Immortality* (Philosophical Library, New York, 1950)

Lampe, G. W. H. and Mackinnon, D. M.   **The Resurrection* (Mowbray, London, 1966)

Lewis, H. D.   *Freedom and History* (Allen & Unwin, London, 1962)
   The Elusive Mind (Allen & Unwin, London, 1969)
   Philsophy of Religion, Teach Yourself series, (E.U.P., London, 1965)

Lewis, H. D. and Slater, R. L.   *World Religions* (Watts, London, 1966)

Lubac, H. De   *The Religion of Teilhard de Chardin* (Collins, London, 1967)

MacIntyre, A. (ed.)   *Metaphysical Beliefs* (S.C.M., London, 1957)

Mackintosh, H. R.   *Immortality and the Future* (Hodder & Stoughton, London, 1915)

McTaggart, J. M. E.   *Some Dogmas of Religion* (Arnold, London, 1906)
   Studies in Hegelian Cosmology (Cambridge U.P., 1918)
   The Nature of Existence, ed. C. D. Broad (Cambridge U.P., 1968)

Major, H. D. A., Manson, T. W. and Wright, C. J.   *The Mission and Message of Jesus* (Nicholson & Watson, London, 1937)

Malet, A.   *The Thought of Rudolf Bultmann*, tr. R. Strachan (Irish U.P., Shannon, 1969)

Manson, T. W.   *Studies in the Gospels and Epistles* (Manchester U.P., 1962)

Martin, J. P.   *The Last Judgment in Protestant Theology from Orthodoxy to Ritschl* (Oliver & Boyd, Edinburgh, 1963)

Marty, M. E. and Peerman, D. G.   *New Theology* Nos 5, 7 (Macmillan, New York, 1968 and 1970)

Mascall, E. L.   *Christian Theology and Natural Science* (Longmans, London, 1956)

Meyerson, E.   *De L'Explication dans les Sciences* (Payot, Paris, 1927)

Milne, E. A.   *Modern Cosmology and the Christian Idea of God* (Oxford U.P., 1952)

Mitchell, B.   *Faith and Logic* (Allen & Unwin, London, 1957)

Montefiore, H.   *Can Man Survive?* (Collins Fontana, 1969)

Morgan, K. (ed.)   *The Path of the Buddha* (Ronald Press, New York, 1956)

Moule, C. F. D. (ed.)   *The Significance of the Message of the Ressurrection for Faith in Jesus Chirst*, Studies in Biblical Theology, Second Series No. 8 (S.C.M., London, 1968)

Niebuhr, R.   *The Irony of American History* (Nisbet, Welwyn, 1952)

Niebuhr, H. R.   *Christ and Culture* (Harper Torch, New York, 1951)

Nineham, D. E.   *St Mark*, Pelican Commentary (Penguin, London, 1963)

Nuttall, G. F.   *The Reality of Heaven* (Independent Press, London, 1951)

Ogden, S.   *The Reality of God and Other Essays* (S.C.M., London, 1967)

Owen, H. P.   *Concepts of Deity* (Macmillan, London, 1971)
   The Christian Knowledge of God (Athlone Press, London, (1969)

Pannenberg, W. *Jesus: God and Man* (S.C.M., London, 1968)

Payne, E. A. *Violence, non-Violence and Human Rights* (Baptist Union of Great Britain and Ireland, 1971)

Pelikan, J. *The Shape of Death* (Macmillan, London, 1962)

Pelikan, J. *Twentieth Century Theology in the Making:* vol. 1: *Themes of Biblical Theology* (Collins Fontana Library of Theology and Philosophy, 1969)

Penelhum, T. *Survival and Disembodied Existence* (Routledge, London, 1970)

Phillips, D. L. *Death and Immortality.* New Studies in the Philosophy of Religion (St Martin's Press, New York, 1970)

Pieper, J. *Hope and History* (Burns & Oates, London, 1969)

Pittenger, N. **God in Process* (S.C.M., London, 1967)

Polanyi, M. *Personal Knowledge* (Routledge, London, 1962)

Quick, O. C. *Doctrines of the Creed* (Collins Fontana, London, 1963)

Radhakrishnan, S. and Moore, C. A. *A Source Book of Indian Philosophy* (Princeton U.P., New Haven, 1957)

Ramsey, I. T. *Biology and Personality* (Blackwell, Oxford, 1965)
   Freedom and Immortality (S.C.M., London, 1960)
   'Hell' in *Talk of God*, Royal Institute of Philosophy Lectures, vol. ii, 1967–8 (St Martin's Press, New York, 1969)

Rawlinson, A. E. J. *Essays on the Trinity and the Incarnation* (Longmans, London, 1928)

Robinson, H. W. *Redemption and Revelation* (Nisbet, London, 1938)
   The Christian Doctrine of Man (T. & T. Clark, Edinburgh, 1911)

Robinson, J. A. T. **In the End, God* (Collins Fontana, 1968)

Rogers, E. *Commentary on Communism* (Epworth, London, 1951)

Rosenstock-Huessy, E. *The Christian Future* (Harper Torch, New York, 1966)

Rupp, E. G. **Last Things First* (S.C.M., London, 1964)

Russell, D. *The Method and Message of Jewish Apocalyptic* (S.C.M., London, 1964)

Schleiermacher, F. *The Christian Faith*, tr. H. R. Mackintosh and J. S. Stewart (T. & T. Clark, Edinburgh, 1928)

Shaw, B. *Back to Methuselah* (Penguin, London, 1965)

Simon, U. *The End is Not Yet* (Nisbet, London, 1964)

Smart, N. *Philosophers and Religious Truth* (S.C.M., London, 1964)
   The Religious Experience of Mankind (Scribner, New York, 1969)

Smith, J. E. *Reason and God* (Yale U.P., New Haven, 1961)

Strawson, W. *Jesus and the Future Life* (Epworth, London, 1970)

Streeter, B. H. (ed.) *Immortality* (Macmillan, London, 1930)

Tavard, G. H. *Paul Tillich and the Christian Message* (Burns & Oates, London, 1962)

Taylor, A. E. *The Faith of a Moralist* (Macmillan, London, 1937)

Taylor, V. *The Gospel according to St Mark* (Macmillan, London, 1952)

Tennant, F. R. *Philosophical Theology*, vol. i (Cambridge U.P., 1928)

Thielicke, H. *Death and Life* (Fortress Press, Philadelphia, 1970)

Tillich, P. *Systematic Theology*, vol. ii (Chicago U.P., 1957)

   Systematic Theology, vol. iii (Chicago U.P., 1963)

   *The Courage to Be (Yale U.P., New Haven, 1959)

Toynbee, A. and others *Man's Concern with Death* (Hodder & Stoughton, London, 1968)

Trethowan, I. *Absolute Value* (Allen & Unwin, London, 1970)

Ulrich, S. *The End is Not Yet* (Nisbet, London, 1964)

Walker, D. P. *The Decline of Hell* (Routledge, London, 1964)

Ward, J. *Psychological Principles* (Cambridge U.P., 1920)

Wild, J. *The Challenge of Existentialism* (Bloomington, Indiana U.P., Bloomington, 1959)

Of the books listed above that are marked with an asterisk, the following are available in American editions:

Clark, *Interpreting the Resurrection*, Philadelphia: Westminster, 1967

Cullmann, *Christ and Time*, Philadelphia: Westminster, 1964

Hick, *Christianity at the Centre*, New York: Herder & Herder, 1968

Joad, *Guide to Modern Thought*, Folcroft, Pa.: Folcroft, 1973

Joad, *Guide to Philosophy*, New York: Dover, 1936

Pittenger, *God in Process*, Naperville: Allenson, 1967

Robinson, *In the End, God*, New York: Harper, 1968

Rupp, *Last Things First*, Philadelphia: Fortress, 1964

Index